THE

LEGACY

OF

B.F.

SKINNER

Concepts

and

Perspectives,

Controversies

and

Misunderstandings

ROBERT D. NYE

State University of New York
College at New Paltz

THE LEGACY OF

Brooks/Cole Publishing Company
Pacific Grove, California

B. F. SKINNER

Concepts

and

Perspectives,

Controversies

and

Misunderstandings

Brooks/Cole Publishing Company
A Division of Wadsworth, Inc.

Printed in the United States of America
10 9 8 7 6 5 4 3 2 1

Library of Congress Cataloging-in-Publication Data

Nye, Robert D.
    The legacy of B.F. Skinner: concepts and perspectives,
  controversies and misunderstandings / Robert D. Nye.
        p.   cm.
    Includes bibliographical references and index.
    ISBN 0-534-16944-9
    1. Skinner, B. F. (Burrhus Frederic), 1904–1990. 2. Behaviorism
(Psychology) I. Title.
BF109.S55N84 1992
150.19'434'092—dc20   91-21644
                                                                        CIP

Sponsoring Editor: *Claire Verduin*
Editorial Assistant: *Gay C. Bond*
Production Editor: *Marjorie Z. Sanders*
Manuscript Editor: *Micky Lawler*
Permissions Editor: *Carline Haga*
Interior and Cover Design: *Cloyce J. Wall*
Cover Photo: *Courtesy of B. F. Skinner*
Typesetting: *Omegatype Typography*
Printing and Binding: *Malloy Lithographing, Inc.*

To Eileen and Jed, for many reasons

PREFACE

B. F. SKINNER and the radical behaviorism that he advocated are very controversial. He left a loyal following, but he also left many opponents who enthusiastically counter his views. There are individuals in both the pro- and anti-Skinner camps who have presented well-informed arguments and perspectives. Still, for many people there remain misunderstandings and misinterpretations about what Skinner was *really* saying. This book is an attempt to help those who are interested (whether laypersons, students, or professionals) to gain a clear understanding of Skinner's legacy: his basic behavioral concepts and perspectives, as well as controversies and misunderstandings regarding his views. It is based on the belief that Skinner's approach, right or wrong, remains lively and timely and provides a real challenge to some of our traditional ways of thinking about human behavior.

The mere mention of the name "Skinner" or the term "behaviorism" can arouse strong emotional responses, often accompanied by comments such as:

> "Skinner? Oh, yes, he's the one who thought that people are like rats in mazes."
> "Skinner believed that people are robots."
> "There's no place for individualism in Skinner's scheme of things."
> "If Skinner had his way, we would all be controlled like puppets by some mastermind who pulls our strings."
> "Skinner didn't take human feelings and emotions into account; he was too coldblooded. Besides, he said that there are no such things as freedom and dignity."

These statements don't accurately represent Skinner's views. Indeed, some of them contain a note of fear or suspicion that can detract from careful consideration of the meanings and possible importance of his proposals, as in the following comments: "Skinner talks about control and says we all are controlled by external conditions. That's enough for me. I'm not interested in controlling or being controlled. I'm interested in being myself and in being free, and that's what I want to know about."

Probably Skinner's widespread public reputation (second only to Sigmund Freud's, if psychologists are being considered) is due in part to the very misinterpretations, oversimplifications, and suspicions that exist. They make his ideas more sensational. Unfortunately, the real nature of his proposals often remains distorted, and their potential benefits are overlooked. With all of the personal and social problems that we face, it seems ill advised to ignore suggestions that might lead to the betterment of our troublesome situations. A closer and clearer look at the actual content of Skinner's proposals is needed to see what potential benefits exist.

My own position with regard to Skinner's radical behaviorism is this: I'm not a completely devoted disciple, but much of what he says makes good sense to me. As I've become more familiar with his writings, I've become increasingly friendly toward his views. My initial reactions to Skinner, after first hearing about him many years ago, were similar to those of many others. I thought his ideas about human behavior were simplistic, that they had only very limited application, and that they were somewhat depressing in their emphasis on how we are controlled by our surrounding conditions. I was much more interested in theories that emphasize the importance of our feelings, thoughts, and expectations as determinants of what we do. Even after I had been a college teacher for several years, and had developed a course comparing Skinner with several other major figures in psychology, I considered his approach rather sterile. I devoted a sustantial part of the course to his ideas and concepts of behavior mainly because of their importance within the field of psychology. Additionally, I felt it was fun and instructive to compare his approach with other influential psychological theories (psychoanalysis, for example).

As the years went by, I continued teaching this course. I read more of Skinner's writings, as well as those of other theorists. Time and again I reviewed these writings as I attempted to respond clearly and specifically to students' questions. Also, I began writing a book, first published in 1975, on the perspectives of Sigmund Freud, B. F. Skinner, and Carl Rogers.* (Rogers is a major figure in humanistic psychology; he is best known as the founder of client-centered therapy.) In concise form I presented the major ideas of these three influential men and then compared, contrasted, and criticized them. It was an interesting experience. As I became involved with each theorist, I found myself "taken over" by that particular view of human behavior. Only after I had finished writing the book did I feel that I could step back and look at each approach objectively.

My thinking about Skinner's psychology has changed over the years. Intensive exposure to his approach, while simultaneously studying alternative approaches, has resulted in an increased appreciation of his concepts. Contrary to

---

*This book is now in its fourth edition: *Three Psychologies: Perspectives from Freud, Skinner, and Rogers* (Pacific Grove, CA: Brooks/Cole, 1992).

my initial impressions many years ago, they seem to apply to a wide variety of human situations and give cause for hope that we can solve some of the difficulties that plague us and our society.

In short, two major thoughts accompanied the writing of this book: a growing sense of the importance of Skinner's work and the awareness that his ideas are often misjudged. I believe that a clear, concise picture of what Skinner said in various writings is necessary so that individuals can decide for themselves whether or not his approach has value. In addition to providing such an overview, this book gives a solid basis for comparing Skinner's concepts with those of other thinkers in the field of psychology and for judging the discussions and comments that abound regarding him and his approach. He is discussed not only in psychology textbooks and college courses but also in popular magazines such as *Time* and *Newsweek* and on TV Talk shows (Skinner himself appeared on Dick Cavett's show and on William F. Buckley's *Firing Line*, as well as on other shows). He comes up in cocktail-party conversations, PTA meetings, friendly philosophical debates, and practically anywhere that ideas are exchanged.

A question that might be asked at this point is: "If someone wants to learn what Skinner had to say, why not simply read his writings?" My answer is: "That would be great, but . . . .." The main qualifications that I would add are: (1) Skinner's ideas appear in over 200 articles and books that he published, "in which he laid out a philosophy, a science, and a technology of behavior" (Vaughan, 1990, p. 101); therefore it isn't easy to "simply read his writings." (2) He sometimes discussed complex behavioral concepts and issues, such as the role of feelings in a behavioral analysis, that are difficult to understand without some preparation; this book helps provide that preparation.

My intention is to inform readers about B. F. Skinner and his approach in a relatively quick and easy (but accurate) way. The material that follows consists of my interpretations of his writings after years of careful study. In various places I've inserted my own examples and expanded on his statements. I believe that these additions help clarify his concepts and provide an accurate picture of important aspects of Skinner's psychology.

It must be remembered, in fairness to the originator, that the final authority on what B. F. Skinner said was Skinner himself. Also, a great deal more was said in his many years of writing than could possibly be included here. Whenever you want to know *exactly* how he expressed his views, or to know the full extent of his comments, there is no substitute for consulting his original writings (many of which are listed at the end of this book). For readers who intend to pursue Skinner's own works, this book serves as an introduction and highlights certain topics. For those who already have read some of his writings, it may provide clarifications, promote reflection, and encourage further reading.

The chapters are arranged in a sequence that seems logical to me. However, they actually can be read in any sequence, depending on the reader's interests and "reading style." Some people prefer to go directly to the subjects that interest them most. The chapters stand independently; that is, each is complete on its own. I do believe that, for the fullest appreciation and understanding of the material, especially for the person who has little or no prior exposure to Skinner's psychology, the chapter sequence makes sense. However, for those who want to "ramble around" among the chapters, there aren't any serious disadvantages to doing so.

ACKNOWLEDGMENTS

WITHOUT THE RESEARCH and writings of B. F. Skinner, this book obviously would not have been written. I appreciate his effects on me and am thankful for the "inspiration" that resulted from reading his articles and books.

My wife, Eileen, again provided support and suggestions, as she did during my previous writing projects. She always has been willing to help, and I am grateful. I also appreciate the many opportunities that our son, Jed, has given me to observe that behavior can defy easy explanations.

During the writing of an earlier, shorter version of this book *(What Is B. F. Skinner Really Saying?,* Prentice-Hall, 1979), several people were especially involved, and I remain thankful for their help. Two of my teaching colleagues, Mark Sherman and Richard Sloan, read and commented on portions of the manuscript. Dr. Sherman's knowledge of behaviorism and Dr. Sloan's nonbehavioristic perspectives were valuable to me. A psychology major and friend, Rose Navarra, contributed her comments and helped sustain my optimism. Larry Wrightsman, of the University of Kansas, provided encouragement during an early stage of my work on the project, and I thank him for helping to make it seem sensible and worthwhile.

Robert Epstein and Fred Keller served as reviewers of the earlier manuscript. Both were closely associated with Skinner and his work, and I benefited greatly from their helpful suggestions, detailed advice, and enthusiasm.

Dr. Epstein, now Director *Emeritus* and Trustee, Cambridge Center for Behavioral Studies, also reviewed the manuscript for the present book. Again he made constructive suggestions; I value greatly his expert opinions. Dr. Richard Rakos, Cleveland State University, was the second reviewer; he contributed careful and detailed comments, which caused me to reconsider several important points in the manuscript.

The staff at Brooks/Cole Publishing Company was terrific during the whole process of completing this project. Claire Verduin, Managing Editor, was totally supportive. Micky Lawler applied her expertise to the editing of the manuscript and reinforced my efforts with her positive comments. Marjorie Sanders, Production Editor, kept everything moving smoothly and efficiently. To them and everyone else at Brooks/Cole who had a part in publishing this book, "thanks."

ROBERT D. NYE

CONTENTS

THREE

FOUR

FIVE

SIX

THE

LEGACY

OF

B.F.

SKINNER

Concepts

and

Perspectives,

Controversies

and

Misunderstandings

ONE

B. F. Skinner: A Brief Biography

SKINNER'S NAME is widely recognized. In one study (Goodell, 1975), 82% of college students could identify him. But does that mean that they really know about the man and his background? Probably not. The following information fills in some of the details of Skinner's life. (The primary sources used when writing this chapter were Skinner, 1967, 1976, 1983b, and 1983c—see the Annotated References at the end of the book.)

Burrhus Frederic Skinner ("Fred" to his friends) was born on March 20, 1904, in Susquehanna, a small railroad town in northeastern Pennsylvania. His mother had trouble with the birth and almost died (this was occasionally brought to Skinner's attention during the following years). His first name came from his mother's maiden name (it was a problem for him because of the necessity of spelling and explaining it). His father was William Arthur Skinner, an attorney with political aspirations who worked for the Erie Railroad for some time; his mother was Grace Madge Skinner, whom Skinner described as beautiful, bright, and, in many ways, the dominant family member; she had strict, unchanging standards.

Physical punishment was hardly a part of Skinner's upbringing. His father never used it, and his mother applied it only once, washing his mouth out with soap for using a bad word. Though reluctant to use physical force, it seems that his parents were not as hesitant in using other methods to bring home the importance of good behavior. William Skinner often told his son about the consequences of having a "criminal mind" (Skinner, 1967, p. 390) and even went so far as to take young Skinner to the county jail to impress him with the facilities there. Also, during one of his summer vacations the boy was taken to a lecture in which life at Sing Sing Prison was described (Skinner admitted that even as an adult he retained a fear of the police). Apparently the importance of such demonstrations was also believed in by Grandmother Skinner, who pointed out to the boy the similarities between Hell and the glowing coals in the parlor stove.

Skinner's mother was very concerned with proper behavior and with what other people might think. A second-grade report card, which noted that he annoyed others, was the cause of considerable upset in the family. He remained bothered by the notion that things had to be "right;" for example, he continued to twinge whenever he cracked the spine of a book—being taught to have respect for books had long-lasting effects. He said that "my parents taught me to fear God, the police, and what people will think," but "I have adjusted reasonably well" (Skinner, 1983c, p. 28).

Skinner's early life seems to have been, in many ways, representative of a typical all-American, small-town boyhood of an earlier time. The earliest possession that he remembered was a teddy bear, and he and his younger brother (his only sibling) played with blocks, toy trains, dominoes, puzzles, checkers, and paper airplanes. Both his mother and his father read stories, such as "Hansel and Gretel," to the boys; his mother also sang to them. He had the usual childhood diseases of the time, including measles, chicken pox, whooping cough, and mumps. As an adolescent he had the customary concerns about the consequences of masturbation.

His home environment was described by him as "warm and stable" (Skinner, 1967, p. 387). His grandparents, whom he saw frequently, provided influences in addition to those provided by his parents. He lived in the same house from birth until just before he left for college (when the family moved to Scranton, Pennsylvania) and attended the same high school from which his parents had graduated. It was a small school with outdoor toilets and no playground equipment. All 12 grades were in the same building; in Skinner's graduating class, there were eight students. He enjoyed school and got a strong grounding in mathematics, Latin, and English; he supplemented his science education by doing experiments at home. He was used to being around books, since his father had a substantial home library.

Outside of his school activities, he enjoyed wandering through the hills around Susquehanna and did the usual things a boy would do in such a setting: swam in the creek, ate berries, killed rattlesnakes, canoed down the river with other boys, and so on. Young Skinner also had a penchant for building and inventing. He built sleds, rafts, bows and arrows, blowguns, roller-skate scooters, wagons, model airplanes, and more; a favorite project was to try to build a glider in which to fly. His inventions included a flotation system for separating ripe from green elderberries and a perpetual motion machine that didn't work. His innovative construction projects continued throughout his life; he had a great ability to change his environment to suit him, and his office was "a labyrinth of switches, pulleys, extension cords, lights, magnifying glasses, cardboard boxes, and cubbyholes connected by strings, rubber bands, masking tape, and hot glue" (Vaughan, 1990, p. 101). Skinner also had musical and artistic interests, playing the saxophone and piano quite well and doing watercolors and charcoal drawings. Even in his later years, a piano, an organ, and a clavichord could be found in his home.

A strong influence on Skinner during his school days was an unmarried teacher named Mary Graves. She had strong cultural interests and was the organizer of a local literary club, the Monday Club, to which Skinner's mother belonged. Miss Graves was Skinner's teacher in a number of classes, including drawing in the lower grades and English later on. She also taught Presbyterian Sunday School classes and took Skinner and a number of other boys through most of the Old Testament. (Skinner's religious training, apparently begun by his grandmother, spanned the years of his early youth, but while still in his teens he became disenchanted with his belief in God.)

A disagreement with Miss Graves about whether or not Shakespeare had actually written *As You Like It* stimulated Skinner, in the eighth grade, to rush to the library and search through various sources to defend the notion that Francis Bacon actually was the author. This undertaking was probably his first real taste of dedicated scholarship. Skinner suggested that it was likely Miss Graves's influence that caused him to become an English literature major in college and, after college graduation, to attempt a writing career.

The decision of where to go to college was not complicated for Skinner. A family friend suggested Hamilton College, a small liberal arts college at Clinton, New York, and that's where he went. He quickly joined a fraternity and proceeded to take "an absurd program of courses" (Skinner, 1967, p. 391). Despite its absurdity, he eventually found it to be of good use to him; as he put it, "No educational counselor would have recommended my program of courses, but at some time or other I have used something from every one of them" (Skinner, 1983c, p. 25). While he majored in English, his other courses included Romance languages, public speaking, and biology, embryology, cat anatomy, and mathematics (he took no psychology courses). He found that what had been considered good standard English in Susquehanna was not considered so at Hamilton, and he had some difficulties learning proper phrasings and pronunciations.

A tragedy occurred at home while Skinner was visiting from college during the Easter vacation of his freshman year. His brother, two and a half years younger, became suddenly and severely ill. The doctor was called quickly, but nothing could be done. At age 16 the boy died from a cerebral hemorrhage. This death had a dramatic effect on the family, but Skinner remained fairly objective about it. The relationship between Skinner and his brother had been noncompetitive in certain ways because of their different interests, but the younger brother had been better at sports, was more popular, and was closer to their parents. As occurs in most families, there was teasing between the brothers, with the older Skinner being the recipient of remarks about his artistic and literary interests. With his brother gone, Skinner became the focus of increased attention within the family, and this position was uncomfortable for him.

During his sophomore year, Skinner met the family of Percy Saunders, the dean of Hamilton College. He was asked to tutor one of Saunders's children in mathematics, and this led to his participation in cultural activities with the family, such as musical events in their home. Through this family he met a young woman who was the daughter of a Utica, New York, banker. He developed a strong infatuation, but the feeling was not mutual and he experienced months of pain and loneliness. His meeting the Saunders family (and, I assume, the related developments) was referred to by Skinner as the most important thing that happened to him at Hamilton College.

During his senior year at Hamilton, Skinner's sexual initiation took place when he and two friends (at their suggestion) visited a house of prostitution in Utica. He later recalled that the experience was brief and not as exciting as he had anticipated (probably because he was hardly at ease in the situation). There were at least two additional occasions on which he and his friends traveled to Utica for the same purpose.

Fitting comfortably into the routine of college life apparently was not Skinner's style, judging from a number of incidents about which he wrote. He had difficulties adjusting to the physical education requirements because of his lack of ability at sports, and he complained about the injustice of such requirements. He and another student pulled off a hoax involving a supposed visit to the campus by Charlie Chaplin; a large crowd (in some 400 cars) gathered in vain at the college to hear the famous actor. Skinner used student publications to attack Phi Beta Kappa (the esteemed national honorary society) and various faculty members. Even Commencement Day was considered fair game, and Skinner and his cronies made such a disturbance during their graduation ceremonies that the college president apparently threatened to refuse them their degrees. They must have settled down sufficiently to satisfy the president, because Skinner did graduate from Hamilton College in the spring of 1926.

During the last term of his senior year, Skinner struggled with the difficult decision of what to do after college. He suggested to his parents that he return to live with them in Scranton, Pennsylvania (where they had moved the year he left for college), and write a novel using that town as the setting. William Skinner responded to his son in a lengthy letter, pointing out the importance of deciding how to make a living and establishing oneself in order to be able to have a home and family of one's own. The father did not totally discourage the son's writing ambitions but gave the usual parental advice about the need to plan for the future. Whatever deterring effect this letter may have had on Skinner's plan to become a writer of fiction was quickly offset by another letter received a short time later. It was from Robert Frost, the noted poet, whom Skinner had met briefly the previous year at the Summer School of English at Bread Loaf, in Vermont. Frost had suggested that Skinner send him some of his work, and he complied by sending three short stories. Frost's response, which came in April of Skinner's last college term, was very favorable. With this push, a writing career was decided upon. After graduation Skinner moved back home and set up a study on the third floor of his family's house.

The first year during which he tried to become a writer did not go well. He thought that a novel was too large an undertaking, so he tried writing short stories—with little success. Very shortly he began feeling that his decision to write was a bad one, and he found that he was distracted easily. He began to be aware of the drabness of his life in Scranton, though he did enjoy reading, attending an occasional concert, working in a local drama group, and so on. He also started thinking about alternatives to writing: chicken farming in California, chauffeuring, and landscape architecture. The last of these he considered after working for a landscape gardener as a laborer for 35¢ an hour; the plan was scrapped, however, when he discovered that he had developed a severe allergy to grass.

Finally, Skinner did manage to get a substantial writing project under way, though it was hardly what he had originally planned. His father suggested to him that he write a digest of the decisions that had been reached by the Board of Conciliation (set up by President Theodore Roosevelt) in its settlements of hundreds of grievances brought by coal companies and unions. The purpose of the digest would be to provide company lawyers with a convenient reference. Skinner tackled the job and found it boring, but it did have its rewards. It gave him experience in classifying facts, and the money he made on *A Digest of Decisions of the Anthracite Board of Conciliation* gave him the opportunity to consider new avenues of activity. (This project gave strong evidence of how Skinner could persevere: He read and summarized 1148 grievances. He showed this tendency again in his later dogged pursuit of behavioral concepts in the experimental laboratory, though in the latter case he certainly had more interest in his work.)

When it became obvious to Skinner that he had failed to become the kind of writer that he wanted to be, he attributed his failure to the literary method itself. He had wanted to investigate human behavior in his writing but now felt that, even though a writer could describe the details of behavior, he didn't necessarily understand the behavior. Skinner decided to turn his attention toward psychology, a field about which he knew almost nothing. In college he had taken no courses in psychology, though some of his reading did border on it.

After beginning seriously to consider psychology as the discipline that he would pursue, Skinner's reading focused more directly on that field. Bertrand Russell's book *Philosophy* came to his attention. In this book Russell spent considerable time on the behavioristic approach of John B. Watson (the founder of behaviorism); though not in fundamental agreement with Watson, Russell nevertheless suggested that there was a good deal of truth in his proposals. This inspired Skinner to buy Watson's book *Behaviorism,* and he moved from a philosophical approach to psychology toward an empirical, scientific approach.

The final confirmation of Skinner's decision to turn from literature to psychology resulted from his reading of an article by H. G. Wells, published in 1927 in the *New York Times Magazine,* in which Wells expressed his admiration for the work of Ivan Pavlov (the famous Russian physiologist who studied conditioned reflexes and thereby made a tremendous contribution to scientific psychology). Thoroughly convinced of his desire to study psychology, Skinner began inquiring about graduate schools. He finally applied for admission to Harvard University and was accepted for the fall of 1928.

Skinner (1967) said that his decision to go into psychology was determined by "many odds and ends" (p. 395). Certainly the events mentioned in the previous paragraph were important, but earlier occurrences also played a part. During his youth he was impressed by the performing pigeons at a county fair, and he always had been interested in animal behavior. For example, he had captured and observed turtles, snakes, chipmunks, lizards, and toads. His father had perhaps stimulated his interest in psychology by frequently calling his attention to interesting bits of behavior, such as the methods baseball players use to deceive the umpire and the unique speech patterns of certain people. Even at an early age, Skinner was curious about any unusual behaviors that he saw. At least some of the roots of his interest in psychology clearly extended back to his experiences as a youngster.

Skinner's acceptance for graduate study at Harvard greatly pleased his parents, and his father suggested that the family take a European trip during the coming summer. Skinner was not overjoyed at the thought of traveling with his parents, but he agreed to go, with the qualification that he would arrive ahead of them and spend a month or two on his own. That still gave him several months before leaving, and he decided to spend the time in Greenwich Village in New York. He had acquaintances there, and he knew something about it from a previous visit. During the months that he spent in the Village before leaving for Europe, Skinner read more psychology (including Pavlov's *Conditioned Reflexes* and Watson's *Psychological Care of Infant and Child*), went to parties, had an affair with a married woman, and worked in a bookstore for $15 a week. The time to go to Europe arrived, and it went as planned: he went ahead of his parents, did some traveling, and met them in Paris. More traveling followed, and then they returned to Scranton. Shortly thereafter, Skinner headed for Cambridge, Massachusetts, and Harvard University.

About his early experiences at Harvard, Skinner (1967) wrote that his interests initially were a "hodgepodge" (p. 397) and that the Department of Psychology had little effect on his sorting out of these interests. Two fellow graduate students, Fred Keller and Charles Trueblood, helped him do that. Keller already was a dedicated behaviorist, and Trueblood (who, like Skinner, previously had been involved in writing) was studying the behavior of rats in mazes. Skinner's courses included psychophysical methods, abnormal psychology, statistics, and German (to satisfy the language requirement). A highly intellectual environment surrounded him, and he had the chance to interact with influential thinkers in psychology as well as related fields. In the fall of 1930, Skinner wrote his doctoral thesis, a study of reflex behavior, and he received his Ph.D. the following year.

Skinner stayed on at Harvard for five years after finishing his doctoral work, being supported by fellowships as he did various animal studies. He was influenced by Pavlov's prescription to "control the environment and you will see order in behavior" (Skinner, 1967, p. 399).

When Skinner's fellowship ended in 1936, the country was in the midst of a severe economic depression. Job prospects looked bleak, but through personal contacts Skinner was offered a teaching position at the University of Minnesota for an annual salary of $1900. He had never taught before and felt that he was keeping only a small jump ahead of his students in introductory psychology. However, he did a very effective job: 5% of his students over a five-year period went on to get Ph.D.s in psychology. He later referred to this period of teaching as richly reinforcing.

In 1936 another important event occurred. Skinner married Yvonne Blue, a former English major from the University of Chicago. They had met through mutual friends only about six weeks before their marriage. According to an article on Skinner that appeared in *Time* magazine (September 20, 1971), she remembers her reaction: "When I met him, he was convinced he was a genius" (p. 53). Yvonne

Skinner shared her husband's strong interest in reading, though he admitted that her reading speed was double his.

The Skinners had two children. The first, Julie, became a professor of educational psychology and has written textbooks in that field; she married a sociologist. The second, Deborah, has been the subject of much public attention and concern. When the Skinners decided to have their second child, Yvonne commented that she felt the first two years of childrearing are difficult. Her husband responded by suggesting that they mechanize some of the required care of the baby. Thus the "baby-tender" was born, along with Deborah Skinner, and she became the famous "baby in a box." Her fame resulted largely from an article with that title published by Skinner in the October 1945 issue of the *Ladies' Home Journal,* in which he reported on the baby-tender and the progress of his infant daughter (also see Skinner, 1979a). The term "Aircrib" later replaced "baby-tender" (another name suggested to Skinner was "Heir Conditioner").

The special crib consisted of an enclosed space with a glass front, through which the baby could watch what was going on around her. Because of the carefully regulated temperature within the enclosure, she had to wear only a diaper; the usual undershirt, nightdress, sheets, and blankets were unnecessary. This was a real benefit because it gave more freedom of movement to the infant and also prevented the development of rashes (it also cut down on the amount of laundry and the continual dressing and undressing that usually must be done). The floor of the Aircrib was covered with a tightly stretched woven plastic sheet, with a texture similar to linen. This sheet was about ten yards long, wrapped on a spool at one end of the crib and emptying into a hamper on the other; this allowed the sheet to be pulled through as it became soiled, a convenient way of providing a consistently clean surface for the baby to lie on. The Aircrib was partially soundproofed, and a shade could be drawn over the glass front.

Despite the fact that Skinner tried to make it clear that there were obvious advantages to using the Aircrib, many people were alarmed by what they considered a cold, unfeeling method of handling (or, rather, *not* handling) an infant. It is true that Deborah immediately went into the Aircrib after she was brought home from the hospital and used it for two and a half years as a sleeping space, *but* it must be remembered that she was able to see out through the glass whenever she was active *and,* very importantly, she was taken out frequently for play and cuddling. She was by no means simply stuck into the crib and forgotten. Even today, however, despite the fact that hundreds of parents (including Skinner's older daughter) have used Aircribs, rumors persist that Skinner was inhumane and uncaring toward Deborah. Furthermore, it is often suggested that she is either psychotic and institutionalized or has committed suicide. (At least once during each semester that I teach, I have to respond to a question something like: "How does Skinner feel about the daughter who went crazy after being kept in a box?" or "Isn't it true that one of Skinner's daughters is psychotic and that the other committed suicide?")

Although a lot of suspicion exists about the outcomes of Skinner's "baby box" procedure, it seems ill-founded. Deborah went to college, studied art in London, and established herself in that field (one showing of her colored etchings was conducted under the auspices of the Royal Academy of Arts). Also, she is married, is interested in a wide variety of music, and could beat her father at chess. (She did break her leg while skiing, but Skinner disavowed responsibility for that.) Deborah herself has suggested that probably the rumors about her, rather than the Aircrib experience, are responsible for any psychological problems that she has had. In the *Time* article referred to earlier, she indicated her belief that criticisms of the Aircrib are based on misunderstandings and that as a baby she was very happy. An article in the June 11, 1979, issue of the weekly magazine *People* (pp. 73–76) also debunks the widespread stories about the supposed negative effects of her experience in the Aircrib; in both words and pictures, her successful life is described.

To get back to Skinner's career, he stayed at the University of Minnesota from 1936 to 1945. His first major work, *The Behavior of Organisms,* was published in 1938 and reported his research with rats. His famous novel, *Walden Two,* was written during the summer of 1945 (it was not published until 1948; he had difficulty finding an interested publisher). Skinner had accepted a position, starting in the fall of 1945, as professor and chairman of the Department of Psychology at Indiana University and therefore had only a short time left in Minneapolis. He felt a variety of dissatisfactions that summer regarding certain common life problems: he wondered whether there could be a better way to deal with situations such as running a household, educating children, finding leisure time to enjoy one's hobbies, and being able to do the kind of work that one finds most satisfying. It seems that having to leave the security of his life in Minnesota to take over the responsibilities of a chairmanship at Indiana University played a part in stimulating Skinner to think about these matters. This move involved uprooting his older daughter from her school, finding new housing, leaving friends behind, and so forth. These types of considerations (plus the urging of a friend who was interested in what kind of community Skinner could suggest as suitable for the future of returning World War II soldiers) led him to write *Walden Two,* a fictional account of a society in which many everyday problems are solved in nontraditional ways. In *The Behavior of Organisms* he had not attempted to apply his laboratory results to the outside world; in *Walden Two* this is precisely what he did attempt to do. It is a story of a community that is run according to concepts of behavioral engineering and of a small group of outsiders who visit the community.

Skinner has said that writing *Walden Two* was a self-therapy venture, in which he was trying to reconcile inconsistencies in his own behavior. On the one hand, Skinner was pursuing a rewarding, but traditional, academic and scientific career. One the other hand, there was a part of him that leaned toward accepting a different approach to life, one that would involve turning his back on the university to try a new, communal-type lifestyle as pictured in *Walden Two.* The university won out, apparently because Skinner would not give up his responsibilities and opportunities to advance behavioral science in the ways that he already had begun. If he had decided otherwise, he might have had to go off to his new life alone. According to comments printed in *Time* (September 20, 1971), Yvonne Skinner was not in favor of giving up what they had to start a communal existence:

"We had tremendous arguments about *Walden Two*. I wouldn't like it; I just like change and privacy" (p. 53).

Walden Two was written in a manner different from Skinner's usual approach. He said that he generally wrote slowly in longhand, producing about 100 words that were publishable for each three or four hours of daily writing. He finished *Walden Two* in seven weeks using a typewriter, sometimes writing very emotionally. He mentioned that one part was typed "in white heat" (Skinner, 1967, p. 403).

After his flurry of activity on *Walden Two,* Skinner arrived at Indiana University to assume the psychology chairmanship. His administrative duties didn't keep him out of the laboratory, as he had feared might happen. He managed to find time to do a number of behavioral experiments, using pigeons as subjects.

In 1947, while giving some special lectures at Harvard University, Skinner was invited to become a permanent member of the Department of Psychology there. He accepted and, after finishing his responsibilities at Indiana in 1948, returned to Harvard. There he amassed a long list of accomplishments, including very successful laboratory research, many years of effective teaching, work on teaching machines and methods of programmed instruction, the study of psychotic behavior at the Metropolitan State Hospital in Waltham, Massachusetts, and the writing of a number of significant articles and books on behavioral concepts and the application of those concepts to social problems.

Skinner officially retired in 1974, but in actuality his association with Harvard went on. For years he regularly walked to his office there to continue many of his activities, including involvement in a variety of new research projects. Also, he continued to do a prodigious amount of writing. His "retirement" was not a time of leisure.

Among the many colleges and universities that acknowledged Skinner's contributions by awarding him honorary degrees are: Hamilton College (his alma mater), University of Chicago, University of Exeter (England), McGill University (Canada), Tufts University, Ohio Wesleyan University, and Western Michigan University. Among his numerous other distinctions are: the Distinguished Scientific Contribution Award of the American Psychological Association (1958); the National Medal of Science (1968); the International Award of the Joseph P. Kennedy, Jr., Foundation for Mental Retardation (1971); the Humanist of the Year Award, American Humanist Society (1972);* and the Award for Distinguished Contributions to Educational Research and Development, American Educational Research Association (1978).

Eight days before his death at age 86 (on August 18, 1990, of complications from leukemia), Skinner gave a brief keynote address at the annual convention of the American Psychological Association (APA) and received a Citation for Outstanding Lifetime Contribution to Psychology. He is the only person in the history

---

*About this award, Skinner (1983b) wrote: "If Humanism meant nothing more than the maximizing of personal freedom and dignity, then I was not a Humanist. If it meant trying to save the human species, then I was" (p. 343).

of the association to receive this award. It certainly can be said that he lived a life devoted to furthering his ideas and that those ideas, however controversial, won him wide recognition.

It is well established that psychologists recognize Skinner's effects on the field. A sample of APA members ranked him the most important contemporary contributor to psychology (Wright, 1970). Also, he ranked second only to Freud in number of citations in a sampling of introductory psychology textbooks (Perlman, 1980). These findings perhaps indicate wide acceptance of the importance of Skinner's basic research and his operant-conditioning concepts. They don't necessarily indicate acceptance of his interpretations of complex human activities such as thought, emotion, and verbal behavior, or of his prescriptions for changing society; there clearly are many psychologists who dispute his ideas on these and other issues. As suggested by Epstein (1987), "On only one matter . . . [regarding Skinner] is there universal agreement and, indeed, praise: Skinner has made significant contributions to the scientific understanding of behavior" (p. 333). On other matters, controversy exists. So that you can come to your own informed opinion about the value of Skinner's approach, his basic concepts *and* his more controversial perspectives are presented in the following chapters.

T W O

Basic Concepts

SKINNER'S PROPOSALS for coping with human problems come from his basic concepts of behavior. They provide the foundation on which he builds. This material will enhance the understanding and appreciation of later chapters, especially for readers who are not familiar with the basics of his psychology. A major reference for this chapter, as well as for certain other portions of the book, is *Science and Human Behavior* (Skinner, 1953).

Fundamental Premises

Boiling Skinner's psychology down to its most fundamental premises, we have: (1) organisms, animal and human, are active—they emit behaviors of various kinds; (2) when a behavior is emitted, it has consequences that may affect the future of the behavior—these consequences may either increase or decrease the likelihood that the behavior will occur again; (3) the consequences are determined by the organism's physical and social environments.

Skinner filled in many details around these simple propositions and told us how various consequences affect our behaviors. He believed that this type of information is essential for understanding why people behave as they do. Though many students of human behavior prefer to look at "the inner person" to find answers to complex human activities, Skinner focused on events in the external environment.

Underlying Assumptions

Beyond the simple premises just stated, there are a number of assumptions that Skinner made in developing his psychology. These will be discussed briefly before we move on to his major behavioral concepts. They constitute a framework characterized by *objectivity, determinism,* and *a concern about practical applications.*

1. *Behavior is lawful; it is determined and controlled in systematic and consistent ways by genetic and environmental factors.*

2. *Genetic endowment determines certain aspects of behavior (for example, the basic types of behavior that we are capable of emitting); however, the effects of environmental factors existing during the individual's lifetime can be observed and altered more directly.* Even though genes influence behavior, the environmental experiences of each of us shape and maintain many behaviors that characterize us as individuals. (A note of caution: A distinction sometimes is made between "genetic" and "environmental" as through the former is completely separate from the latter. It must be remembered, however, that Darwin's theory of evolution suggests that genetic endowment is determined by environmental conditions. The species members who behave in ways that allow survival in their environments are the ones most likely to produce offspring, thereby perpetuating their particular genetic—and behavioral—characteristics. Skinner pointed out the importance of past environments in selecting behaviors by referring to "contingencies of survival.")

3. *The role of psychology is to discover the "cause-and-effect" relationships between environmental events and behavior.* (To be precise, cause-and-effect connections in scientific studies are commonly referred to as "functional relations." Though scientists may reveal the effect that one event has on another, they are cautious about implying that they know *how* the event causes its effect. Therefore, Skinner considered the phrase "functional relations" to be appropriate. He suggested, however, that the terms "cause" and "effect" can be used informally.) The field of psychology has the special task of investigating the effects of environmental events on behavior. Other scientists, such as those involved in studying physiology, eventually may be able to tell us specifically what occurs inside the body when we behave. This will be valuable information. However, since knowledge of the relationships between environmental events and behavior always will be crucial, psychologists should vigorously pursue their own specialty.

4. *The best method for determining critical relationships is to control specific environmental conditions ("causes") and observe the resulting behavioral outcomes ("effects").* This is the "experimental method" and is quite different from the kinds of observations that we make in everyday life (which are usually "uncontrolled" observations, meaning that all sorts of unknown factors can be affecting the behaviors we are looking at, thereby making it difficult or impossible to determine the critical factors). With the experimental method, specific conditions can be arranged deliberately and the resulting changes in behavior observed.

5. *Studies of lower animals are useful in determining basic behavioral concepts that can then be tested out at the human level.* The main advantages of studying rats, pigeons, and other lower animals is that they are simpler than humans, their past histories and present circumstances can be controlled more easily, and they can be studied over longer periods of time under specified

conditions. Though humans obviously are different from lower animals in their behavioral capacities, there is no reason to reject the possibility that the same behavioral concepts apply to both. (In fact, considerable evidence indicates that various concepts *do* apply to both.)

6. *Behavioral concepts derived from the experimental study of relationships between environmental events and behaviors can be applied to human problems.* Findings from both animal and human studies can be used to improve human conditions. They can be brought out from psychologists' laboratories into the real world, applied to real-life situations, and monitored carefully to determine their effectiveness. (This approach, which has been used effectively in many cases, is called "behavior modification" or "applied behavior analysis.")

7. *It is unnecessary and misleading to speculate about feelings, thoughts, or other "inner states" as causes of behavior.* Such states certainly do occur, but these internal, bodily conditions do not control behavior. Environmental conditions (for example, reinforcement or punishment) influence these inner responses as well as overt behaviors. In other words, feelings, thoughts, and other inner states can be considered effects rather than causes. (This is perhaps the hardest aspect of Skinnerian psychology to accept, since we are so used to attributing our actions to our feelings and thoughts.)

Operant Behavior

Skinner was interested primarily in behaviors that have effects on the physical and social environments within which we live. He saw humans as active organisms, capable of emitting a wide variety of such behaviors. Behaviors that "operate" or act on the environment to produce consequences, and are in turn affected by these consequences, are called *operants;* changes in behaviors due to their consequences is the process of *operant conditioning.* The consequences determine whether we do the same thing (or something similar) again. Certain outcomes strengthen the behaviors that precede them, whereas others do not. The multitude of behavioral consequences that occur during our lifetimes shape our behaviors into what they are at any given point in time. To use a non-Skinnerian word, these outcomes determine an individual's own unique "personality."

The study of operant behavior is at the core of Skinnerian psychology, so much so that often it is referred to as "operant behaviorism." Skinner's operant behaviorism should be distinguished from earlier forms of behaviorism such as that of John B. Watson, who generally is considered the first behaviorist in the field of psychology (his writings on the subject began to appear in 1913). Watson paid considerable attention to the findings of Ivan Pavlov, the famous Russian physiologist who gave us Pavlovian (or classical) conditioning.

It is not unusual to read or hear comments that equate Skinner's and Pavlov's interests. However, they are very different. The work for which Pavlov is famous concentrated on the study of relatively simple, reflexive-type responses. For example, many people have heard of the studies in which he trained dogs to salivate to the sound of a tone. After being paired repeatedly with the presentation of food, the tone by itself elicited salivation. Thus an initially neutral stimulus (a tone) became a conditioned stimulus. The dog was relatively passive in this conditioning process. It was strapped into a harness-type apparatus, and the salivation reflex was elicited by presenting food slightly after the tone was sounded. In Skinner's studies, as you will see, more active responding is required for conditioning to occur.

The conditioning of a reflexive response (such as salivation) to an initially neutral stimulus (such as a tone) has important implications. Watson believed, and suggested in a very dramatic study (Watson & Rayner, 1920), that emotional responses such as irrational fears can be explained by Pavlovian conditioning. By pairing the presence of a white rat (an initially neutral stimulus) with a loud noise (a frightening stimulus), he conditioned an infant to fear the rat. Before it had been paired with the loud noise, the animal elicited no fear responses from the infant. (Though Watson's findings, published in 1920, are important, serious questions remain about his procedures, the ethics of having conducted such research, and interpretations of the study. With regard to the last point, it seems that operant conditioning, as well as classical conditioning, was involved.)

Skinner acknowledged the significance of Pavlovian conditioning (he called it "respondent conditioning") for interpreting responses that are *elicited* by initially neutral stimuli. However, his main interest was *emitted* responses, which make up most of the important activities that we engage in, such as reading, studying, writing, working, playing sports, developing hobbies, talking to each other, and so on. None of these consist primarily of elicited, reflexive-type behaviors; rather, they consist mainly of *operants*. In this emphasis, Skinner differed from Watson's earlier focus on Pavlovian conditioning, and he proceeded to devote himself to the study of operant conditioning by focusing on emitted behaviors, their consequences, and surrounding conditions.

It should now be clear that Skinner's psychology is *not* a stimulus-response (S-R) approach, even though it often is portrayed as such. Whereas Pavlovian conditioning can be labeled an S-R approach, because a stimulus *elicits* (or draws out) a response, in operant conditioning a response must be *emitted* before it can be reinforced. Skinner studied what commonly are considered to be "voluntary" behaviors.

Skinner might best be considered an "S-R-S" psychologist (Epstein & Skinner, 1982, p. 2). He *was* concerned with stimuli, but not in the eliciting sense. This will be made clearer later on; for now it is sufficient to say that he was "concerned with (1) the circumstances under which behavior occurs (the first 'S'), (2) the behavior itself (the 'R'), and (3) the consequences that the behavior produces (the second 'S')" (Epstein & Skinner, 1982, p. 2). As will be explained later, the relations among these three things constitute "contingencies of reinforcement."

The Skinner Box

To pursue his interest in operant behavior, Skinner built a small, soundproof chamber that provides an experimental space within which an animal can be studied. This type of device commonly is referred to as a *Skinner box,* though Skinner himself avoided calling it that (among the expressions that he used are "experimental space," "experimental apparatus," "experimental chamber," and "operant chamber"). In this chamber an animal can be isolated from interfering influences and subjected to specific conditions created by the experimenter. The operant behaviors that typically are studied are lever pressing by a rat or the pecking of a small disk (called a "key") by a pigeon. When sufficient pressure is applied to the lever or the key, a food dispenser is triggered and a food pellet or grain (which serves as a reinforcer for lever pressing or key pecking) is made available. The animal's presses or pecks are recorded electromechanically over a space of time, with the rate of response being the datum that is of primary interest.

Various environmental conditions can be produced by an experimenter to see how each condition affects the animal's response rate. For example, how frequently does a rat press the lever if a food pellet is delivered after each response, when compared with a condition in which food appears after every 15 responses? In simple terms, such studies indicate how hard an animal will work under different conditions of reinforcement. Another question might be "If an animal has been trained to respond at a high rate though reinforcment of its responses, how long will it take for the animal to stop responding when reinforcers are no longer available?" This can be studied by establishing a period of time during which food pellets are delivered when a rat presses or a pigeon pecks, and then cutting off the food supply until the animal "gives up" on that response. By doing innumerable studies of this kind, in which conditions are varied in specific detail, Skinner and his colleagues collected a vast amount of data on how environmental events affect the frequency of behaviors.

Important questions often arise when Skinner-box studies are discussed: "What do they have to do with *our* behavior?" "How can lever pressing and key pecking be related to the behaviors that *humans* engage in?" These questions can be answered in at least two ways. *First,* Skinner looked for basic behavioral concepts, and these concepts can be discovered in their purest forms by studying organisms that are relatively simple and easy to control experimentally. The relative isolation provided by the Skinner box helps keep the situation itself simple by ruling out all sorts of possible interfering influences on the animal's behavior. *Second,* the concepts that are discovered by studying lower animals can be tested at the human level. In other words, Skinner didn't suggest that rats and pigeons are exactly the same as people. Rather, he believed that there are certain similarities among living organisms and that behavioral processes found at one level may well apply at other levels.

Once a process is known to occur with rats or pigeons in a Skinner box, we are in a position to move to more complex levels and check on its validity in the world populated by people. In fact, this is what has happened with Skinnerian procedures. Many studies have shown that they can be applied effectively in education, industry, business, government, prisons, mental institutions, and family settings. They don't always work easily or perfectly, but often they can be tailored to fit particular situations so that substantial benefits are obtained, such as increases in efficiency and productivity, better interpersonal relationships, and decreases in undesirable behaviors.

What Skinner and his colleagues have done is similar to what goes on in other sciences, such as physics, chemistry, biology, and medicine. Researchers in these fields often study phenomena in the artificial environments of their laboratories, hoping to produce findings that will apply under real-world conditions. Medical researchers, for example, often use lower animals to test drugs or procedures before applying them to humans.

A comment needs to be made regarding the use of *rates of response* as the basic data collected by Skinner and other behaviorists who have followed in his footsteps. In Skinner-box studies (as well as in studies of human behavior in real-life settings), these data allow comparisons to be made of the effects of different conditions. The actual behaviors that are counted in the Skinner box (that is, pressing or pecking) are used simply because they are convenient to measure and they occur reliably. There is nothing especially significant about these particular responses as far as Skinnerian psychology is concerned—other responses with similar characteristics could be used. The *rate* of response, however, is more critical. Given some thought, it becomes clear that many assumptions made about both animals and people are based on the frequency with which specific behaviors occur. For example, our assumptions about someone's attitudes, interests, habits, or preferences are often based on how frequently we observe that individual do certain things. Isn't it important, then, to understand the various conditions that cause increases or decreases in what organisms do? This is what Skinner studied.

Reinforcement

The most important of Skinner's behavioral concepts is *reinforcement*. The term indicates a *strengthening effect* that occurs when operant behaviors have certain consequences. Behavior increases in probability (that is, the likelihood of its occurrence under similar circumstances increases) when its outcomes are reinforcing. A food-deprived rat whose lever pressing in a Skinner box is reinforced with food pellets presses the lever again and again.

Though it is common practice (even in some psychology books) to substitute the term "reward" for "reinforcement," the two are *not* necessarily the same. Rewards may or may not strengthen behavior. For example, a teenager may behave contrary to his parents' wishes, despite the fact that they heap rewards (a car, money, freedom, and so on) on him. These parents are giving rewards to their son, but they aren't *reinforcing* his desirable behaviors.

By Skinner's definition, reinforcement *does* strengthen behavior; reinforcement is occurring *only* if what is being done has that effect. Although so-called rewards may strengthen behavior (in which case they are also reinforcers), they do not necessarily do so. Another point is that in general usage we often speak of "rewarding a good person," but using Skinner's approach we speak of "reinforcing good behavior." The latter emphasizes the importance of consequences (especially immediate consequences) for specific behaviors; also, it is behavior (not the person) that is strengthened.

It should be noted that Skinner's use of the term "reinforcement" is primarily descriptive; that is, it describes a relationship between a response and an environmental event. Specifically, it refers to an occasion when behavior is strengthened because it is followed by some stimulus (or, to put it another way, some consequence); the stimulus itself is called a "reinforcer," and its delivery is called "reinforcement." The concept of reinforcement describes only the fact that certain consequences strengthen behavior; it does not explain *why* this occurs.

What generally is strengthened when reinforcement occurs is not just a particular response. A "class of responses" is strengthened, and the term "operant" applies to this class. Suppose that a boy's polite request for a dollar is immediately reinforced by his mother giving him money, "Polite requesting" is the operant behavior that is strengthened, and it consists of more than just one particular response pattern. In other words, the boy's behavior is more likely to be polite on future occasions when requesting money, but the "politeness" may take somewhat different behavioral forms. Similarly, when a rat's lever-pressing response is reinforced with a food pellet, that *exact* response may not be repeated; other responses (operant behavior) that result in the bar being pressed may be emitted and reinforced. In essence, then, an operant (or operant behavior) consists of those responses that produce a given consequence; the responses may vary somewhat, but they have the same result.

Sometimes people fault Skinner's reinforcement procedure by saying "I've tried it and it doesn't work!" The problem in such cases may relate to what was said earlier: reward, but not reinforcement, may have been used. You can't always find a "reinforcer" easily. Although money, gifts, praise, and so on often do work as reinforcers, in some cases they do not. Something else may be necessary. For example, a parent may find that simply listening carefully to a son or daughter, or spending some leisure time together, reinforces desirable behaviors to a greater extent than does the giving of rewards.

You can't always be sure what will be reinforcing, since differences sometimes exist from person to person, from behavior to behavior, and from situation to situation. You can be sure that reinforcers are being used only when the relevant behavior is being strengthened. In other words, reinforcers are determined empirically; the effects must be observed to determine if reinforcement is occurring. Also, as indicated before, it is very important to make reinforcers contingent on specific behaviors, rather than simply "rewarding the person."

Getting back to the relatively simple situation of the lever-pressing rat in a Skinner box, at first glance this might seem only to provide a mildly interesting demonstration of how an animal's behavior can be controlled by reinforcing it. However, for Skinner and his followers, this simple form of operant conditioning is an elementary example of a behavioral process that applies across species and has tremendous significance for explaining human behavior. Skinner's early studies of rats provided him with findings that he guessed would apply at the human level, and subsequent research by many behavioral psychologists has given considerable support to the idea that the behavior of people, as well as that of pigeons and rats, is controlled by the consequences of their actions. Although we usually don't receive food pellets, our behaviors are dramatically affected by other reinforcers such as money, compliments, sex, public attention, and approval from others. Our actions also are often reinforced by the direct environmental changes they produce: reaching for an object produces contact with it, approaching something brings us closer to it, turning toward someone makes him or her visible, and so on. Of course, the complexity of situations, behaviors, and reinforcers among humans is extremely different from that existing in a Skinner box. Nevertheless, the Skinnerian assumption (which is suggested by a large amount of evidence) is that some of the most basic behavioral concepts (such as reinforcement) are the same.

An outstanding illustration of the effects of reinforcement on human behavior has been provided by the well-known writer Isaac Asimov:

> Most people seem to fear and resent behaviorist notions. They seem to think it denies man freedom of will and makes of him merely a machine. I heard William Buckley discuss *Beyond Freedom and Dignity,* a book by B. F. Skinner, and he referred to Skinner's theories as implying "a dehumanization" of man. But does behaviorism dehumanize a man or merely *describe* a man?
>
> Frankly, I tend to accept behaviorist notions. I find the behavior of people quite predictable; and the better I know them, the more predictable I find their behavior. People sometimes surprise me, I admit, but I have the feeling that this is because I don't know enough about them and not because they are capable of free will.
>
> And, of course, my own behavior is most predictable of all; at least, to me. For instance, I respond favorably to praise. It has an extraordinary reinforcing effect on me. All my publishers and editors find this out at once. It is their profession, of course, to study the weaknesses of writers and use those weaknesses to manipulate those writers. So they carefully begin to praise the quickness with which I complete my work; the speed with which I read galleys and prepare indexes; the cooperativeness with which I make (reasonable) revisions, and so on and so on.
>
> All this I lap up with avidity; no one has ever handed out praise in larger servings than I can swallow. What's more, in order to get still more of it, I complete my work more quickly than ever, read galleys and do indexes with still greater speed, make *reasonable* revisions with at least a trace of a smile, and the result is that over the last six years I have averaged nine books a year.
>
> Came the time when I was supposed to work on the introductions to these chapters. I was in New York; the editorial staff was in California. I sent off some introductions and heard nothing. Whereupon I grew sad and sulky and found that I didn't feel like doing any more. When I was nudged very politely by the editors, I wrote a long letter, saying that unless I knew that they liked those I had already written, I could do no further work. Whereupon the staff, suddenly enlightened, promptly sent me a letter telling me that my introductions were great and that everybody loved them. At once I sat down to write more. Periodically, they sent me kind words and I sent more introductions. It was very neat and efficient.
>
> But does that mean I'm just a robot? That I have buttons that need pushing? That I point them out, that they push them, and that all is well? Well, I guess so. I

like to be praised and that's what I work for. Maybe we all have our buttons, and maybe we all know where they are, and maybe we all do our best to get them pushed.

Could the behaviorists be saying that it's love that makes the world go round?*

The effects of reinforcement during our lifetimes mold our behaviors along certain lines. When we learn how to swim, ride a bike, throw a ball, sew, sweep a floor, drive a car, and so on, the successful (reinforced) responses are the ones we continue to make. The unsuccessful responses tend to drop away. The same process holds true for our social behaviors at work, school, and home. For example, speaking and dressing in acceptable ways bring approval from employers, teachers, parents, peers, and others. Approval and other social reinforcers are very significant influences. Whether we consider physical or social activities, the effects of reinforcement are critical.

Positive Reinforcement and Negative Reinforcement

In operant conditioning there actually are two types of reinforcement. So far, we have been discussing *positive reinforcement:* a response is strengthened by the *addition* of something to the situation. The "something" that is added is called a *positive reinforcer.* A rat pressing a lever for food pellets, a worker doing a job for money, a student studying to get good grades, a child "being good" to earn parental approval, and even a person pulling on a doorknob to open a door are all examples of the effects of positive reinforcement. The positive reinforcers are, respectively, food pellets, money, good grades, parental approval, and an open door.

Behaviors are strengthened not only by positive reinforcers, however. Many actions that allow us to escape or avoid negative consequences also become part of our typical behavior patterns. When this happens, our behavior is being conditioned by *negative reinforcement:* a response is strengthened by the *removal* of something from the situation. In such cases the "something" that is removed is referred to as a *negative reinforcer* or *aversive stimulus* (these two phrases are synonymous). We already have seen that a hungry rat's lever pressing can be strengthened by positively reinforcing that response with food pellets. We could also accomplish this by using negative reinforcement. If lever pressing removes a painful electrical charge (which can be a negative reinforcer or aversive stimulus), it is very likely that the rat will soon be conditioned to make that response whenever it receives a shock through the floor grid of the Skinner box.

The phrase "negative reinforcement" can be confusing, so consider it very carefully. Remember, it refers to a process whereby behavior is *strengthened,* not weakened. Often it is confused with "punishment," which will be discussed

---

*CRM Staff, *Psychology Today: An Introduction,* 3rd ed. (New York: CRM/Random House, 1975), p. 68.

shortly. Whereas negative reinforcement results in an *increase* in the probability of behavior, punishment typically acts to *suppress* behavior; this is an important distinction.

Skinner suggested that negative reinforcement is a very influential determinant of behavior. Many examples exist: the child who does his chores to stop his parents' nagging, the parent who gives in to her child's demands in order to stop temper tantrums, the student who cuts classes to avoid a teacher's reprimands for poor performance, the wife who escapes her husband's tirades by going into the bedroom and locking the door, the driver who obeys speed limits to avoid being ticketed, the person who gets drunk to escape from stressful life situations, the person who takes aspirin to stop a headache, and so on. Nagging, temper tantrums, reprimands, tirades, speeding tickets, stressful situations, and headaches are *negative reinforcers* or *aversive stimuli* in these examples. Their removal is reinforcing, and therefore the behaviors that remove them tend to become conditioned.

In Skinner's opinion, it is unfortunate that so much of our social behavior is influenced by *negative* reinforcement. In an improved society we would be controlled more by *positive* reinforcement. In other words, instead of escaping and avoiding aversive stimuli, it would be better to be positively reinforced more of the time. A couple of examples illustrate the point. Schools have often relied on threats of failure or disciplinary actions to spur slow students to study hard, rather than teaching the subject matter clearly and in sufficiently small steps so that making progress could be reinforced (this results partly from teachers being burdened with too many students to allow individual instruction). Employers have often counted on the fact that their employees will work in order to escape the negative consequences of unemployment, poverty, and deprivation, rather than attempting to provide conditions and jobs that are positively reinforcing.

A sign of an inefficient and poorly planned society, according to Skinner, is a heavy reliance on negative reinforcers to control behavior. The emphasis should be on positive reinforcement. One major reason for this is that the outcomes of positive reinforcement are more predictable than those of negative reinforcement. Undesirable behavior often gets strengthened by negative reinforcement. For example, a teacher might attempt to get a student to study harder by continually criticizing her, and the student might respond by doing more studying. If this stops the teacher's criticisms, studying will be negatively reinforced and the teacher's goal will have been achieved (the student's studying behavior is strengthened because it removes the aversive stimulus of criticism). However, less desirable outcomes are quite possible. The student might escape and avoid the teacher's criticisms by becoming a truant, rather than by studying. Another possibility is that the student might become very withdrawn and spend a lot of time daydreaming in order to cut herself off from the full impact of the criticism.

The main point of these examples is that using *negative* reinforcers such as criticism to control behavior may result in the reinforcement of unwanted behaviors. On the other hand, using *positive* reinforcers is more likely to give the desired result. There is nothing to escape or avoid in a positive-reinforcement situation. Therefore, alternative behaviors that are undesirable are less likely to be emitted and reinforced.

To summarize briefly, there are two different types of reinforcement: positive and negative. In both types, behavior is strengthened. In positive reinforcement the consequence of behavior is the *addition* of something (a positive reinforcer) that increases the probability of the behavior. In negative reinforcement the consequence of behavior is the *removal* of something (a negative reinforcer or aversive stimulus) that increases the probability of the behavior. Skinner advocated using positive, rather than negative, reinforcement to control behavior.

Primary Reinforcers and Conditioned Reinforcers

Some positive reinforcers, such as food, water, and sexual contact, are related to our basic biological functioning. These are called *primary reinforcers*. There also are negative reinforcers that are considered primary: electrical shocks, pin pricks, hard blows, extreme cold or heat, and so on. Both positive and negative primary reinforcers have a significant effect on how we behave. However, to understand Skinner's suggestion that a whole array of complex human behaviors can be controlled by reinforcement, it is necessary to consider *conditioned reinforcers*.

A conditioned reinforcer is a stimulus that is originally neutral but gains the power to reinforce through its pairing with one or more primary reinforcers. Let's look at a Skinner-box example. Suppose that, when a rat presses the lever, a light is rigged to go on when the pellet of food (a primary reinforcer) drops into the food tray. The pairing of the light with food occurs 50 to 100 times. Next, the situation is changed so that neither the light nor food appears when the lever is pressed, and gradually the rat's responses decline to a very low frequency (this process is called *extinction*). At this point it is arranged for the light to go on again when the pressing response is made but for the food pellets to remain undelivered. What will happen to the response rate? Will the light by itself serve as a reinforcer, causing the lever pressing to increase again? As it turns out, the lever-pressing response in such a situation does increase in frequency, showing that the originally neutral light stimulus has become a positive reinforcer—or, more accurately, a positive *conditioned* reinforcer. In cases when the light has not been previously paired with food, it does not have the effect of increasing the response rate.

At the human level there are innumerable examples of conditioned reinforcers. Perhaps the most dramatic is money. Money is associated with many necessities (primary reinforcers) and therefore serves as a reinforcer itself in a multitude of situations. Think of all the behaviors that are controlled by these pieces of paper or metal—there is little doubt about money's reinforcing characteristics.

Signs of affection, approval, or attention from others—which involve certain statements, facial expressions, and body movements—also provide examples of powerful conditioned reinforcers (however, the possibility exists that certain of these signs may be primary reinforcers, due to their evolutionary significance). These signs have a great influence on us, deriving from their many associations with primary reinforcers. Starting at birth, certain verbal and physical behaviors by parents consistently accompany the giving of basics such as food, liquids, warmth, and cuddling. In later life, signs of approval, affection, and attention continue to be associated with primary reinforcers, including sexual contacts. Conditioned reinforcers that are associated with more than one primary reinforcer are referred to by Skinner as *generalized reinforcers*.

Perhaps the most significant point about conditioned reinforcers, especially those that are generalized reinforcers, is that they eventually function independently in a variety of situations to control behavior. We often behave in ways that will yield money or signs of acceptance, approval, or attention from others, even when primary reinforcers are not immediately available. We often work long and hard, or change our behaviors dramatically, to keep these conditioned reinforcers coming, as illustrated earlier by Isaac Asimov's comments. Misers are an extreme example; their behavior is almost completely controlled by money, even though they seldom use it to buy primary reinforcers.

There also are *negative* conditioned reinforcers. For example, an academic grade of "F," the facial expression that we call a frown, the verbal statement "I don't like you," or the sight of a dentist's drill may be stimuli that are aversive because of their past associations with basic deprivations or pain. We tend to behave in ways that allow escape from or avoidance of these aversive conditioned stimuli.

A discussion of reinforcers must include what Skinner believed to be another important influence on human behavior: the positive reinforcement of successfully manipulating the environment—that is, "being effective" or "being right." He suggested that this type of reinforcement is very basic, perhaps related to the genetic makeup of the species. It seems reasonable to assume that those of our ancestors who were most effective in coping with their environments were also the most likely to survive and pass on their characteristics to later generations. Through evolution, then, effectiveness has come to be a powerful reinforcer of human behavior. This idea is very significant, since it suggests that much of what we do may occur partly because we simply are producing environmental changes. In other words, perhaps there doesn't have to be any direct or obvious gain in what we do; rather, our behavior may be positively reinforced simply by producing an effect. (Skinner gave the example of a baby who persistently shakes a rattle, with little to be gained except producing a small environmental change.) This may, in part, explain activities such as gardening, certain artistic pursuits, and sporting activities such as bowling and billiards, which we often say we are doing "just for the fun of it."

A final point to be made in this section is that it can be dangerous to assume too much about the ability of various stimuli to reinforce the behaviors of different individuals. Although certain reinforcers—such as money, words of praise, or a smile—tend to have a great deal of generality, what is reinforcing to one person may not be reinforcing to another, a reinforcer that works in one situation may not work in another, and different behaviors may require different reinforcers. Skinner indicated that a stimulus, to be considered a positive or negative reinforcer in a particular case, should be tested and its effects observed. In other words, does the stimulus actually serve to increase the frequency of the behavior that either *produces* it (in the case of positive reinforcement) or *removes* it (in the case of negative reinforcement)?

In practical applications—for example, in trying to change the behavior of a child, a student, an employee, a spouse, a friend, an acquaintance, or anyone else—it is essential that the process include stimuli that are actually reinforcing, not stimuli that are simply thought to be reinforcing. If you try to reinforce the behaviors of a vegetarian with a steak dinner, an extremely active child with the opportunity to read a book, a beer drinker with a glass of expensive wine, or a solitary person with an invitation to a big party, you are not likely to produce the effect that you intend.

Superstitious Behavior

Typically, operant conditioning involves the strengthening of behavior when reinforcement is dependent on that behavior. There is an "actual" connection between response and reinforcer. Suppose, however, that an *accidental* connection occurs; that is, a reinforcer follows a response but is not dependent on that response. This also results in operant conditioning; the behavior that is strengthened by this process was referred to by Skinner as *superstitious behavior.* He believed that many human actions are "superstitious."

Using pigeons as subjects, Skinner demonstrated the basic processes involved in the conditioning of superstitious behavior. A food-deprived bird is put into the Skinner box. The food dispenser is set to deliver food every 15 seconds, regardless of what the pigeon is doing. Notice that the delivery of food is not dependent on a particular type of behavior. Whatever the animal is doing at the time the reinforcer (food) arrives will be reinforced and therefore will be more likely to be occurring when the next reinforcer comes. In this way, a certain response pattern is built up. With this procedure Skinner conditioned pigeons to turn regularly in circles, thrust their heads high into an upper corner of the cage, and show other unusual movements.

What do humans do that can be traced to processes similar to "accidental" reinforcement in the Skinner box? Rain dances are a classic example. The occasional accidental connection between the dancing and the occurrence of rain provides sufficient reinforcement to keep the practice going. As another example, it has been said that some ancient peoples had a special ritual to deal with eclipses, which apparently they viewed as a giant dragon's attempt to devour the sun. By creating as much noise as they possibly could, they would cause the dragon to release the sun. Assuming that this story is true, it would be an example of accidental *negative* reinforcement—the dragon's threat was an aversive stimulus that was removed (supposedly) by the response of making lots of noise.

In modern society there also are plenty of superstitions. When an athlete prepares for a performance, all sorts of peculiar movements are apt to occur regularly. Each baseball player, for example, has his own special routine when he comes to the plate: tapping the plate with the bat, hitching his pants up several times, touching the peak of the batting helmet in a certain way, and so on. Presumably the player's movements have been developed over time as they have been followed by the reinforcement of getting a hit. Recently I noticed that a player with a good hitting streak came to bat with someone else's protective helmet. He stood fidgeting in the batter's box, stepped in to hit, stepped out again, took off the helmet several times to check it, and finally was rescued by the bat boy who had found the player's own helmet. Comforted, he smashed a solid hit to the outfield—another reinforcement for wearing that particular hat!

Many of us have superstitious ways of dealing with machines. Elaborate routines for starting our cars sometimes develop (especially as the car gets older and becomes harder to start), despite the likelihood that only a couple of the things we do are really effective. We may go through the same routine regularly because these responses, at one time or another, have been accidentally reinforced. Now we continue them, because "The car starts, doesn't it?" The same kind of thing can be seen in the ways we deal with finicky typewriters, TV sets, radios, door locks, electrical switches, and so on. If some behavior "works," even if it really isn't what is producing the reinforcing outcome, we tend to do it again.

Superstitious behaviors can develop in social situations too. A person who puts on a particular type of clothing or rearranges his or her hairstyle and then has a good time at a party or other social occasion may continue to do these things, even though other people were not reacting at all to these aspects of the person. Certain physical gestures and ways of speaking also can become conditioned behaviors when they are followed by reinforcing attention from others, regardless of whether or not the attention is actually produced by these specific behaviors.

Skinner has suggested that, even when strong superstitious behaviors do not result from accidental connections between responses and reinforcers, we can be affected in less dramatic ways by these events. He used the example of finding a ten-dollar bill in the park. Walking in the park and looking down did not actually produce the money, and it certainly isn't likely that money would be found there again even if the individual went to that spot every day. Nevertheless, if money is a reinforcer for that person, it is now more likely that he or she will stroll that way and look downward as was done when the money was found. The person's behavior has been changed, at least slightly, by accidental reinforcement.

It can be difficult at times to determine whether or not a behavior is superstitious. I have two acquaintances who respond in opposite ways to minor illnesses, aches, and pains. One of them goes to a doctor immediately and often receives some medication or medical advice that is followed by recovery (in other words, seeking medical advice is followed by reinforcement). The other person does not go to the doctor, takes no medication, and does nothing special, but also recovers shortly. Perhaps it would be unfair to call the first person superstitious, since going to the doctor is an acceptable and encouraged practice in our society (what people commonly consider superstitious depends heavily on cultural patterns). Also, it might be that going to the doctor actually is advisable for this particular individual's problems. The possibility remains, however, that his seeking medical advice may not be causally related to recovery.

An area of contemporary life that is very touchy in discussions of superstitious behavior is religion. Are various religious beliefs and practices superstitious? A common response to this question probably is something like "Yes—all except mine!" Obviously, Skinnerian psychology cannot provide a final answer here, since considerations of ultimate purposes and supreme powers take place at a different level of discourse. From a strict naturalistic and scientific point of view, however, most religious rituals could be considered "superstitious."

Operant Extinction

To this point, we have been discussing the strengthening of operant behaviors—that is, the ways in which responses are increased in frequency. Now we will discuss how operant behaviors are weakened, or decreased in frequency. Suppose that, repeatedly, nothing happens after a response is made. What then? In operant-conditioning terms, *extinction* occurs: the response eventually decreases in frequency.

Consider a case in which behavior has been strengthened through reinforcement, and then reinforcement is no longer available. The lever pressing of a rat in a Skinner box has been conditioned by presentation of food pellets as a consequence of the behavior. If reinforcement no longer occurs (the food dispenser is disconnected), the rat's lever pressing will eventually stop (or almost stop); that is, it will *extinguish*. (It is important to note that in extinction there may be a *temporary* increase in the frequency of a response before the decrease begins.)

Extinction is another important concept for understanding human behavior. The often-asked questions "Why doesn't she do that anymore?" or "Why has he stopped doing that?" often could be answered if changes in the consequences of the person's behaviors were known. The hardworking executive is likely to become "lazy" if his or her efforts no longer bring praise, promotions, or pay increases; your friendly, good-natured neighbor may no longer give you a warm smile and a big hello if you have been too busy in recent weeks to be friendly in return; you may stop trying to call an acquaintance who never is home to answer the phone. Each of these instances involves a lack of reinforcement for behavior, with the result that the behavior decreases in frequency. Often, the decrease occurs very slowly, and it takes a long time before the behavior completely ceases. More will be said about extinction shortly.

Punishment

Another possible consequence of behavior is *punishment*. "Negative reinforcement" and "punishment" often are confused, but these two concepts are very different. Whereas negative reinforcement strengthens behavior, punishment typically suppresses behavior. Skinner suggested two ways in which a response can be punished: by *removing a positive reinforcer* or by *presenting a negative reinforcer* (aversive stimulus) as a consequence of the response.

Here is an example of how negative reinforcement and punishment differ, using electrical shock as the negative reinforcer or aversive stimulus. If a rat presses a lever to *remove* the shock, lever pressing is negatively reinforced and is strengthened. On the other hand, if pressing the lever *produces* the shock, lever pressing is punished and is likely to be suppressed. In both situations the shock is a negative reinforcer, but in the case of negative reinforcement it is *removed* and in the case of punishment it is *presented.* Some common examples of punishment in which a negative reinforcer is added as a consequence of behavior are: a child who is scolded for swearing, an employee who is reprimanded for arriving late for work, and a driver who is ticketed for illegal parking. Sometimes the physical environment provides punishment for behavior: the infant who touches a hot stove, the bicyclist who takes a painful fall for "showing off," and the jogger who tries to run too fast and pulls a muscle are all experiencing "natural" negative reinforcers.

As mentioned previously, another type of punishment involves the *removal of positive reinforcers.* Children who have their allowances taken away for bad behavior, employees who have their pay reduced for arriving late, and drivers who have their licenses suspended for speeding are examples. Positive reinforcers—allowance, pay, and the right to drive—are taken away as a consequence of certain behaviors.

An interesting point about the term "punishment," as it commonly is used in our society, is that so-called punishments often do *not* suppress the undesirable behaviors at which they are aimed. Ticketed speeders often continue to speed, jailed criminals often continue their antisocial behaviors, reprimanded students often continue doing poorly, and spanked children often continue misbehaving. We deceive ourselves in many such instances by thinking that "punishing" the offenders is effective. A stricter definition of punishment would focus attention on the effects of the punishing actions. In other words, do these actions *actually* suppress undesirable behaviors? If not, does it pay to continue their use?

Skinner generally was strongly opposed to the use of punishment and expressed his opposition on many occasions. He believed that punishment does not have a permanent effect (unless it is extremely severe, in which case it also commonly disrupts or stops desirable, as well as undesirable, behaviors and causes fear, anxiety, resentment, or other problems). Although punishing someone may temporarily cause him or her to stop behaving in an undesirable way, the behavior is likely to reappear, especially when the punishment is withdrawn. Therefore, it is ineffective in the long run and is an inefficient way to get rid of unwanted behaviors.

Other objections to using punishment are: (1) rather than simply stopping the undesirable behavior, punishment may result in other behaviors that are equally undesirable, such as running away, counterattacking, or complaining; (2)

emotional by-products such as fear, guilt, or shame may be produced, and these emotions may be felt whenever the person is around the punisher or the situation in which he or she was punished—for example, the harshly punished student may experience emotional distress whenever he or she is in the classroom; (3) punishment indicates only what a person should *not* do and doesn't give information about what should be done.

If there are so many undesirable aspects of punishment, why is it used so frequently? Skinner suggested that punishment often gives immediate, if not long-lasting, results. In other words, using punishment is often negatively reinforced; something aversive to the punisher is removed. For example, physical or verbal abuse directed at someone who displeases us often causes the displeasing behavior to stop, even if only for a brief time. This is especially true if the person is in a subordinate position to us.

To sum up, using punishment is dangerous because it is habit forming for the punisher, is not a long-range solution, and has undesirable side effects. Does that mean that it should *never* be used? Skinner made very strong arguments against the use of punishment, but he did acknowledge that there are exceptions. For example, it has been found that the self-mutilating behaviors of autistic persons sometimes can be suppressed by administering an electric shock or other aversive stimulus (this may be preferable to using drugs or restraining devices). Once the self-destructive behaviors are halted, there may be an opportunity to reinforce more positive behaviors. Although granting that the limited use of punishment may be necessary at times, Skinner (1988) added: "To remain satisfied with punishment without exploring nonpunitive alternatives is the real mistake" (p. 22). In other words, though it is difficult to avoid totally the use of punishment, we should search diligently for ways of implementing positive reinforcement as a replacement.

Aversive Control

Along with his general condemnation of punishment, Skinner also was against what he called *aversive control.* Whereas punishment is designed to stop behavior, aversive control involves getting others to do something by threatening, explicitly or implicitly, that aversive consequences will occur if they don't do as requested. In simple language, this is a case of "Do it, or else!" The effectiveness of aversive control depends on negative reinforcement; the person does what is requested in order to escape or avoid the aversive stimulus of threat. However, as will be seen below, behaviors other than those expected may get reinforced.

Skinner believed that this type of control should be avoided for some of the same reasons as punishment: its outcomes are not as predictable as those of positive reinforcement, and by-products such as hostility, apathy, anxiety, or stubbornness may develop. The spouse who is threatened with verbal or physical abuse may remain away from home because of the negative reinforcement of getting away from the threats (or, if able, may launch a verbal or physical counter-attack); the employee who is harassed by a supervisor may find it reinforcing to stay home "sick" or to get back at the supervisor by using sabotage techniques; the child who is intimidated at home may run away because of the reinforcement involved in escaping the constant threat of punishment; and many more examples could be given. Instead of producing the expected behaviors—being a "good" husband or wife, working hard on the job, behaving properly at home, or whatever—attempts to use aversive control may backfire. Even when the purpose of getting someone to behave in a certain way is accomplished, the person subjected to threats is likely to show negative emotional reactions, and this may be an outcome that the controller will not be pleased with for long.

Despite all the possible things that can go wrong when aversive control is used, it occurs frequently at all levels of society, from interpersonal relationships to governmental regulations. Skinner explained this disturbing fact: As with punishment, aversive control is often effective immediately. If the person or institution using it is powerful, it will usually work—*at least temporarily*—before the ill effects begin to show.

Skinner favored a shift toward greater use of positive reinforcement for long-range benefits. If a person's behavior is reinforced, he or she will do more of it without the necessity of direct or subtle threats. To go back to our previous examples, spouses are less likely to stray if at home they find enjoyable activities, attention, affection, and satisfying sex; employees are likely to work harder if their efforts are given quick and direct recognition; and children are likely to behave better if their good behaviors are given attention and approval by parents. In these positively reinforcing ways, behaviors can be controlled more effectively than by using aversive control that relies on threats to get people to do what is expected of them. The effects of positive reinforcement may not be as immediate or as dramatic as those of either punishment or aversive control, but they are more likely to be long-lasting and less likely to generate undesirable actions and negative emotional states.

Controlling Problem Behaviors

If Skinner was generally opposed to punishment as a way of stopping behaviors, what did he suggest? One possibility is extinction, a procedure that involves ignoring unwanted behaviors. For example, a parent may simply not pay attention to a child's whining or outbursts of temper. The basic idea is to avoid providing any reinforcement for such actions. If no reinforcement is available, extinction should occur.

According to Skinner, the effects of extinction are more permanent than those of punishment. Though sometimes there may be a brief recurrence (called "spontaneous recovery") of a behavior that has undergone extinction, extinguished behavior tends to remain at a low level of frequency. Unfortunately, however, the extinction process itself may produce emotional responses such as aggression or frustration. Before extinction has finally occurred, there may be vivid displays of these or other problem behaviors. (As will be indicated shortly, it pays to reinforce desirable behaviors while extinguishing undesirable ones.)

There are other difficulties as well. Skinner warned that the process may take a long time. Therefore, the undesirable behavior may have to be endured beyond the limits of the controller's patience while extinction is taking place. For example, having to put up with a number of temper tantrums (while simultaneously trying to ignore their existence) can be very difficult, even if they are gradually decreasing in frequency. Another problem is that there may be an increase in the undesirable behavior for a time immediately following the start of the extinction procedure. If a child's whining usually has been reinforced by the parents' attention, when they no longer provide that attention the whining is apt to intensify. Commonly, it will eventually extinguish, but the temporarily intensified demands may be hard for the parents to put up with, and they may be very tempted to give in; if they do give in, they will reinforce the child's heightened whining behavior.

Another disadvantage of extinction is that it cannot be applied easily when undesirable behavior results in harm to the person himself or to others. For example, extremely aggressive behavior cannot simply be ignored; something must be done to prevent it from occurring. Further, there must be sufficient control over the entire situation to prevent other persons from reinforcing the behavior that you are trying to extinguish. To use the example of the whining child again, an extinction procedure won't be effective if a relative, neighbor, or friend continues to respond to the child's unpleasant behavior.

Skinner admitted that he didn't have all the answers about how to cope with annoying, dangerous, destructive, or otherwise harmful activities. However, he did have a suggestion that can be applied in cases in which simple extinction is not likely to be effective. He advised using a method that reinforces *incompatible* behavior. If a behavior that is incompatible with the problem behavior can be conditioned through the use of positive reinforcement, it is likely to replace the problem behavior. For example, in addition to ignoring whining and temper tantrums, parents should make sure that they pay attention to the child's more reasonable demands. In this way they may be able to shape up more polite and cooperative behaviors. If they are successful, these more desirable responses will become the typical behaviors of the child, replacing the whining and temper tantrums.

This method of extinction combined with reinforcement of incompatible behaviors is an important procedure for use in prisons, delinquent homes, and other institutions to which serious offenders are sent for rehabilitation. This method has strong possibilities. The basic idea is to set up the situation so that no reinforcements are available for the criminal or delinquent activities that have become typical response patterns for the offenders, while providing positive reinforcement for constructive behaviors such as learning job skills, studying, and communicating better with others.

Implementing such programs is much easier said than done. One of the obvious difficulties is getting rid of the possibilities of reinforcement for undesirable behaviors such as fighting, the use and selling of drugs, and sexual attacks. Unless there is sufficient control over the total situation, such activities are likely to continue. On the other hand, complete control may be oppressive and defeat the rehabilitation process. In any case, it seems essential that opportunities for genuinely useful and constructive activities be available and that reinforcers be given for socially desirable behaviors. In many cases, programs don't provide sufficient opportunities for reinforcement of alternative, productive behaviors that actually will be useful in the world outside the institution.

Skinner strongly advised that we look for good alternatives to punishment as ways of controlling behavior throughout society. He cautioned that punishment is too often the easy way out. It often gives immediate results, and therefore we are deceived into believing that it is effective. At best, it is only a temporary answer, giving relief to the punisher as long as he or she is able to hold a threat of more punishment over the head of the violator. When the punisher or the threat is absent, the unwanted behavior is likely to recur, sometimes with a vengeance. The beaten child, the jailed criminal, the reprimanded employee, the severely disciplined student—there are many examples among such individuals of punished behavior that is repeated, sometimes in extreme fashion, when the chance arrives. According to Skinner, it is far better to find ways of applying positive reinforcement for "good" behaviors than to wait until "bad" behaviors occur and then rely on punishment. In his opinion, all social institutions should be structured so that persons systematically receive positive reinforcement for desirable behaviors. This would alleviate the need for the widespread use of punishment, because people would be conditioned to behave in individually and socially beneficial ways.

Considering the three major concepts of Skinnerian psychology that have been discussed so far—reinforcement, punishment, and extinction—where do we stand in trying to explain human behavior? If we think of a person's life from birth to adulthood, we realize that the number and variety of behaviors emitted are tremendous. However, each person develops a unique set of behaviors that becomes common for her or him and that in large part determines that individual's "personality." How do these particular behaviors get selected as the typical ways of responding, when so many other behavior patterns would have been possible? Skinner provides us with an answer. Some of the things we do are *reinforced* (either positively or negatively), and we continue them. Other behaviors have been *punished* and tend to be suppressed, at least under certain conditions. Still other behaviors have been *extinguished* and appear seldom or never. What gets reinforced, punished, or extinguished differs in various social settings. For example, aggressiveness may be reinforced in one society or family and punished in another. This helps to account for cultural and individual differences in behavior patterns.

Basically, this is the kind of broad analysis that Skinner's psychology provides. In this form, the analysis is still somewhat crude and may not satisfy someone interested in understanding the finer points of human behavior. Some of the more subtle details need to be introduced, and this is our next objective.

Generalization and Discrimination

When a response is reinforced in a particular situation, *generalization* (or *induction*) may occur; that is, the response may then be emitted in similar situations. "When we have once brought behavior under the control of a given stimulus, we frequently find that certain other stimuli are also effective" (Skinner, 1953, p. 132).

If generalization didn't occur, our behavior would have to be conditioned again in each new situation, even if the situation were similar to a previous one. Obviously, this isn't necessary. We behave in similar situations on the basis of conditioning in particular situations. A person who drives one car also can drive similar cars. A child who behaves appropriately at the family dinner table also can behave properly at other dinner tables. Many situations have similar stimuli, and it is in the presence of these stimuli that we respond in ways that have been reinforced in the past. Generalization provides the advantage of "ready-made" responses in a variety of settings.

Skinner used the following example to demonstrate generalization: if a pigeon is conditioned to peck a red spot, it will then also peck (at lower rates) an orange spot or a yellow spot, and spots with some variation in shape and size. (If the color was sufficiently different—for example, green—then the pigeon would not be likely to peck.) A *generalization gradient* operates: responding tends to decrease in frequency as the stimuli become increasingly different from the initial stimulus (in this case, a red spot).

Despite its advantages, generalization isn't always a good thing. For example, though driving other cars is possible once one car has been mastered, similar responses may be disadvantageous if one car has an automatic transmission and the other has a manual transmission. Here is where *discrimination* saves the day, if it occurs before an accident happens. Our responses become more finely tuned to different aspects of similar situations. This occurs when similar responses are not reinforced: shifting a manual transmission in the same way as an automatic will not work. Since automatic-transmission movements aren't reinforced, they eventually extinguish and are replaced by the reinforced manual-transmission responses. In brief, then, the process of discrimination involves altering the probability of responses in various stimulus situations, and basically it is the opposite side of the coin from generalization. Both processes are important in everyday life.

Skinner demonstrated discrimination at a simple level by extending the previous pigeon example. As mentioned, once the bird has been conditioned to peck a red spot, the pecking generalizes to an orange spot. However, if reinforcement is changed so that it occurs *only* when the red spot is pecked, and never in the presence of orange, the pigeon eventually stops responding to the orange spot—discrimination has resulted. To give another example: if lever pressing by a rat is reinforced with food pellets when a light is on, but not when it's off, the lever eventually will be pressed only when the light is on. To sum up, discriminations occur when the pigeon pecks only if the spot is red, the rat presses only if the light is on, and the driver shifts gears himself only if there is a manual transmission.

In these examples, the red spot, the light, and the manual transmission have become discriminative stimuli. In their presence, responding in particular ways has been reinforced. Discriminative stimuli exert considerable control over human behavior. Phones are answered only when they are ringing, strangers are approached more often when they are smiling than when they are frowning, and we drive through intersections only when the traffic light is green. The phone's ring, the stranger's smile, and the green light are discriminative stimuli—making the appropriate responses when these stimuli are present has been reinforced (someone usually has been on the line, strangers generally have been friendly, and we have moved through many intersections easily and safely). A whistling teapot is an interesting example: it is a discriminative stimulus signaling the availability of boiling water but soon becomes an aversive stimulus that is reduced when the pot is picked up.

The powerful influence that discriminative stimuli have on our lives is difficult to grasp unless some thought is given to it. Stop for a moment and think about how often your behavior is controlled by particular conditions (often we are so predictably controlled that we call our behaviors "habits"). Skinnerian psychology maintains that the environment is a major determinant of our behavior and that we do not "choose" or "decide" to act in certain ways on the basis of some inner knowledge. Rather, the environment *selects* certain responses. Though we may feel that we are "freely deciding," for example, to approach a smiling stranger, Skinner maintained that both the decision and the approach are affected by the environmental conditions that we have experienced. In other words, the fact that approaching smiling strangers typically has been reinforced with returned friendliness is what determines *both* our decision and the approach behavior. It is not the decision that controls whether or not we will approach the person.

The type of generalization discussed at the beginning of this section sometimes is referred to more specifically as "stimulus generalization." It should be mentioned that "response generalization" also may occur when a particular behavior is reinforced: other similar behaviors may be strengthened. "The reinforcement of a response increases the probability of all responses containing the same elements" (Skinner, 1953, p. 94). If it were not for this phenomenon, each small variation in behavior would have to be reinforced in order to develop a fairly rich behavioral repertoire. Response generalization is not completely understood at this time (nor is stimulus generalization); sometimes behaviors that appear to have little resemblance to the reinforced behavior are strengthened (Kazdin, 1989, pp. 48–50). Nevertheless, the concepts of stimulus and response generalization contribute importantly to a behavioristic interpretation of human behavior by emphasizing the spread of the effects of reinforcement across stimulus conditions and behaviors.

Shaping

Most of the things we are able to do aren't conditioned by a one-shot process. Rather, they are conditioned through the process of *shaping*. Eating with utensils, using tools properly, playing sports skillfully, learning to read, write, and speak a language, as well as many other abilities, develop in steps. Each bit of progress made toward the final behavioral goal is reinforced, but we have to keep moving toward that goal in order to keep the reinforcers coming. For example, very young children are praised for simply picking up a fork or spoon, but shortly they have to pick up food with it to gain their parents' attention. Next they have to hold it correctly, and finally they have to be able to get the food neatly into their mouths to receive approval. Step by step this process goes on, with reinforcement being given for progress and then being held back until more progress is shown.

Skinner suggested that language is conditioned in this way also. Utterances that vaguely resemble words are given attention and praise at first, and then progressively improving performance is required for further reinforcement. In this way the child's verbal behavior is *shaped* until the language can be spoken in an acceptable way. Skinner (1990a) noted that the human species underwent a "unique evolutionary change when its vocal musculature came under operant control and when vocal behavior began to be shaped and maintained by its reinforcing consequences" (p. 1206).

Endless examples of the shaping of constructive human behaviors could be given, but one more will suffice for now. Consider the skilled craftsperson and the way in which his or her highly refined techniques develop. As an apprentice, small improvements in skill are reinforced, perhaps both by the comments of a master craftsperson and by the actual physical effect that the correct behaviors have on the materials being worked with. As time goes on, more and more improvements in technique have to be made in order to produce the desired effect and to earn the recognition of others, until finally the behaviors are very skilled.

Unfortunately, shaping can also have undesirable outcomes. For example, we may unknowingly shape annoying behaviors in others by ignoring (extinguishing) reasonable behaviors and reinforcing louder, more insistent actions with our attention. The parent who doesn't pay attention to the child's quiet requests, and then begins listening when the demands are intensified, may be paving the road toward loud, disturbing behavior. This kind of process happens in many different situations and is suggested by the common expression "The squeaky wheel gets the grease."

Violent, destructive behaviors also can be the result of shaping. For example, if a disadvantaged or oppressed group's reasonable demands are ignored by those in power, more intense demands are likely to result. These may bring some reinforcement in the form of concessions by the authorities. When this level of action no longer is attended to, the group may again escalate its efforts and thereby gain further advantages. If this step-by-step process continues, the end result may be violence, because that is what the group finally has to do to keep the attention of the authorities. This is similar to what happened in the 1960s as Blacks and students escalated their methods of protest. Those in positions of authority would seem well advised to respond to moderate, reasonable requests for the correction of injustices, rather than waiting until they find themselves in the position of having to reinforce violent or disruptive actions.

As with other Skinnerian principles, shaping can be demonstrated in the relatively simple confines of a Skinner box. The lever-pressing rat and the key-pecking pigeon usually do not begin these behaviors suddenly. In other words, they don't simply go over and begin working on the lever or the key. They are led to these behaviors through shaping. For example, reinforcers (food pellets) may be given at first to the rat when it simply is at the end of the Skinner box where the lever is located. Then reinforcement is given only when the rat gets closer to the lever, and so on. When the animal is in the immediate vicinity of the lever (because that is where reinforcement has led it), it will sooner or later make a movement that involves touching the lever, and that response is then reinforced. Next, only responses that put pressure on the lever are reinforced, and so on, until actual pressing occurs and is reinforced a number of times.

By reinforcing behavior that is in the direction of the desired response (pressing the lever) and then withholding reinforcement until an even closer approximation of the desired response is made, the experimenter gradually leads the rat toward lever pressing. After this operant-conditioning process has taken place, on later occasions the food-deprived animal will press the lever very soon after being placed into the Skinner box. A new operant behavior has been conditioned by using a shaping procedure.

In real life, shaping processes do not necessarily work smoothly to produce the best final behavioral products. Earlier, examples were given of using eating utensils, speaking a language, and developing skilled craftsmanship. However, since many of our behaviors are shaped in unplanned and unsystematic ways by parents, teachers, peers, work supervisors, and others, the results frequently are less than desired. Several things can go wrong: (1) if a relatively crude response receives too much reinforcement, it may become so strong that more advanced responses do not occur—for example, parents may give so much attention to a child's early social behaviors that the child fails to develop more mature social responses (the child is "spoiled"); (2) if too-rapid progress is attempted (the step to the next behavior required for reinforcement is too large), existing behavior may be extinguished before more advanced responses are emitted, thereby undoing the shaping that has already taken place—for example, a teacher may "expect too much" from a student and withhold approval for such a long time that the student's academic behaviors begin to decline rather than improve; (3) reinforcement for an advanced behavior may come too slowly, allowing other behaviors to occur in the meantime—the reinforcement may then strengthen these behaviors instead of the desired one (in other words, the wrong behaviors get reinforced)—for example, recognition that a worker gets long after completing an excellent job actually may reinforce poorer performances that have occurred in the meantime. Given the delicacy of the perfect shaping process, is it any wonder that we're so imperfect?

Programmed Material and Teaching Machines

Skinner gave considerable attention to the development of better techniques for shaping behavior. He suggested that many types of learning can be improved by the systematic application of good shaping procedures, and he was instrumental in planning the use of *programmed material* and *teaching machines*. Constructing a "program" involves breaking down the subject matter into small units. This ensures that the learner will be able to make progress and not get stuck at a particular level because the next step is too hard. In small sequential steps, the learner moves toward better and better mastery of the material (mathematics, science, specific job-related information, or whatever). Each effective step in learning the material is reinforced.

There currently are programmed textbooks that present material in small progressive steps. Also, various *teaching machines* are in use. These devices present programmed material in mechanically or electronically controlled ways. A unit of material is displayed, the learner is required to make a response that shows understanding of the material, and feedback is given regarding the correctness of the response (if the program being used is a good one, the learner almost always will respond correctly). A teaching machine can provide the advantages of: (1) keeping the learner busy—there are no long delays during which the learner must sit and wait for more information; (2) allowing the learner to move along at his or her own pace; (3) permitting complete mastery of each unit before the next one is presented; and (4) providing immediate reinforcement of correct responses by letting the learner know he or she is correct. Skinner suggested that there are strong similarities between teaching machines and the private tutor who makes sure that the student understands the material thoroughly, presents material for which the student is prepared, and provides quick reinforcement for correct responses. A good teaching machine and a good tutor are both effective shapers of behavior.

In addition to these advantages, Skinner indicated that teaching machines relieve teachers from the role of "drillmasters," remove the need for aversive control (for example, students do not have to be threatened with low grades), and reduce needless competition among students. It was his belief that tremendous potential exists in the use of techniques based on programmed instruction. One of the difficult problems is designing good programs—that is, breaking down various complex subjects into small, yet meaningful, units. This often is a tough job.

Schedules of Reinforcement

Once behavior has been shaped, it can be maintained by various patterns of reinforcement. Depending on the particular schedule, we may respond slowly or rapidly, show long pauses between responses, persistently respond despite the fact that out behavior hasn't been reinforced in a long time, and display other variations.

The two broad categories of schedules are *continuous* and *intermittent*. With the former, each response of a particular type is reinforced; in the Skinner box, each time the rat presses the lever, it gets a food pellet. With the latter, reinforcement occurs less than each time; for example, only every fifth lever press may be reinforced.

Regarding human behavior, the physical environment is much more likely to provide a schedule of continuous reinforcement than is the social environment. The outcomes of turning water faucets and pushing doors, and more complex behaviors such as riding a bicycle, swimming, hitting a golf ball properly, or hand-weaving a rug, are all activities that deal with physical objects and have predictable outcomes. If these behaviors are performed in particular ways, reinforcement will occur each time. Although social situations are less likely to provide continuous reinforcement, there are exceptions. An acquaintance may always respond in a friendly way to your greetings, certain relatives may always give help when you request it, a certain person may always laugh at your jokes, and so on. Often, however, there is less consistency than this in our interactions with other people, and our social behaviors don't get reinforced every time.

Interestingly, when continuous reinforcement is interrupted, we often feel that something strange, disturbing, or perhaps humorous is going on. Skinner used the example of the "house of mirrors" in an amusement park. The usual feedback is changed and we find it funny. Also, we may wonder or say something like "Isn't that odd?" if someone who has always been friendly suddenly ignores us. More seriously, we may experience severe "self-doubts" if we have been effective consistently in our efforts at school, on the job, or elsewhere, and suddenly some effort is not reinforced. In this situation, the person who is used to "ups and downs" (intermittent reinforcement) is not as apt to feel as discouraged as someone whose behavior has been reinforced continuously.

Extinction tends to occur relatively quickly if a behavior that has received continuous reinforcement is no longer reinforced. Assume that you are used to having a light come on every time you throw a switch. If it doesn't come on one day, you are more likely to give up quickly than if you are accustomed to a finicky switch that sometimes works and sometimes doesn't. In other words, continuous reinforcement leads to faster extinction than does intermittent reinforcement. This holds in social situations too. The person who has a long history of successes mixed with failures in forming friendships is apt to continue trying to relate to people even after a series of unsuccessful attempts. On the other hand, someone who has always made friends easily may give up if a few recent attempts have met with failure. One explanation for the differences in the behaviors of these two persons might emphasize inner qualities such as the greater "diligence" or "persistence" of the first individual. However, Skinner would say that the different reactions result from different schedules of reinforcement.

The fact that behaviors that have been maintained on a continuous schedule extinguish more rapidly than those on an intermittent schedule can be demonstrated vividly in the Skinner box. A pigeon may peck the key 50 to 100 times after reinforcement has been cut off if it previously was on a schedule of continuous reinforcement. After some types of intermittent reinforcement, the bird will peck from 4000 to 10,000 times before responding extinguishes. Anyone who has tried to extinguish some human behavior after having reinforced it intermittently may have experienced these long-lasting effects. For example, parents who try to extinguish their child's temper tantrums may find it frustrating and exhausting, especially if in the past they sometimes gave in and sometimes resisted. For extinction purposes, at least theoretically, it would have been better if they had always given in, rather than just sometimes.

A few examples of human activities maintained by intermittent reinforcement are: writers who continue to produce even though their works are published infrequently; anglers who go fishing time after time but who catch fish only once every several times; gamblers who continue to play games of chance despite only occasional winnings; moviegoers who see film after film but only now and then see a good one; and friends who continue seeing each other despite the fact that it isn't always reinforcing to be together. Lots of behaviors persist when they are reinforced only occasionally. (These examples are intended to illustrate a point; however, actual situations may be more complex. Reinforcers other than those mentioned may be operating. For example, a writer's efforts may be reinforced by the manuscript pages completed, an angler's outings by the sight and smell of the lake and woods, and so on.)

There are two major types of schedules of intermittent reinforcement: *interval schedules* are based on passage of time, and *ratio schedules* are based on number of responses. On an *interval schedule,* the first response after an interval of time has passed is reinforced. Responses made before that go unreinforced. For example, you must wait an interval of time for water to boil before your response of pouring it on instant coffee will be reinforced. Also, checking your mailbox will not be reinforced with letters unless you wait an interval of time since the last mail delivery.

Intervals between reinforcement can be *fixed* or *variable,* and this is an important distinction. Our behavior will usually differ on these two types of interval schedules. On *fixed-interval* (FI) schedules, we tend to wait until the time when reinforcement will occur and then begin our responses. If you always use the same pot, the same amount of water, and the same intensity of flame to boil the water, you have created a fixed-interval schedule. You probably will go calmly to the stove once, after the fixed interval has passed, and find water that's ready to be used. On the other hand, if you use different pots and different amounts of water and turn the flame on carelessly, you will have a *variable-interval* (VI) schedule. Each time you boil water, you are likely to be running back and forth to the stove, checking to see if it's boiling.

Another good example of how FI and VI schedules can make us behave differently is this: Suppose that you are driven to work by a fellow employee who consistently arrives in front of your house at 7:30 A.M. (for our purposes this can be considered a fixed-interval schedule—the interval is exactly 24 hours long). Would your behavior differ from a situation in which your ride arrived sometimes at 7:30, sometimes at 7:39, other times at 7:21, and so on? Probably it would. On this variable-interval schedule, you would probably go to the window a number of times, checking to see if the person had arrived. Someone watching you would probably say that you were nervous, restless, or fidgety, but Skinner would say that your behavior was being affected by a variable-interval reinforcement schedule.

In the laboratory, different results from fixed-interval versus variable-interval reinforcement schedules can be shown dramatically. For example, a pigeon on an FI schedule tends to pause after being reinforced and then accelerates its pecking as the interval draws to an end and reinforcement again becomes available. On a VI schedule, the pigeon tends to maintain a constant rate of pecking, with little pausing. Skinner gave the example of birds on a VI schedule with an average interval of five minutes (the intervals varied around the five-minute mark, sometimes shorter, sometimes longer). They pecked for up to 15 hours, two or three times per second, with almost no pauses except to consume their reinforcers.

Ratio schedules yield reinforcers on the basis of number of responses made (time is not a factor). The important element is the ratio of reinforced to unreinforced responses. These schedules also can be *fixed* (FR) or *variable* (VR). On FR schedules, a certain number of responses is required for reinforcement (for example, a rat may have to press the lever 20 times to get each food pellet). On VR schedules, the number of responses required for reinforcement varies around some average (for example, the *average* number of required lever presses may be 20, but sometimes the numbers may be 15, 40, 1, 24, and so on—essentially, the probability of reinforcement for any particular response remains constant).

Response patterns again differ on these two types of schedules. On FR schedules, typically there are short pauses after reinforcement, followed by rapid responding. Provided the ratio is not too high, fixed-ratio reinforcement yields a high response rate. With large ratios there may be a significant period of slow responding after reinforcement. If the ratio is very large, there may be a long period of no response after reinforcement. Skinner used the example of a student who finds it difficult to start work on the next assignment after finishing a term paper. The fact that a lot more work is required before the next reinforcement occurs not only affects the student's behavior, but he or she may also report feelings of low morale or lack of interest.

The classic example of a fixed-ratio schedule at the human level is piecework: the worker gets paid a certain amount for each unit of work completed. Skinner said that this can be a dangerous schedule because workers may become exhausted; since higher response rates yield more frequent reinforcement, there is a tendency to work harder and harder. He suggested, for example, that it is too tough for salespersons to work solely on commission (which can be similar to piecework); they should have some salary to supplement their commission, or else they may wear themselves out (or, more accurately, the FR schedule will wear them out). The response pattern of animals in the Skinner box can also be seen with humans who are on FR schedules (with ratios that are not too high). They tend to pause briefly after being reinforced (for example, after completing a unit of work) and then work hard again until the next reinforcer occurs.

Variable-ratio schedules also can result in a high rate of activity, and pauses tend to disappear. Skinner indicated that pigeons will peck for hours at a rate of five times per second on this type of schedule. An example frequently used by him to illustrate the dramatic effects that a VR schedule can have on human behavior is that of pathological gamblers. They make bet after bet, any of which might pay off. The outcome of any particular bet is unpredictable, but eventually they win (unfortunately, this occasional reinforcement keeps the gambler going, even when the overall outcome is disastrous). Variable-ratio schedules abound in our lives: calling our friends, playing games, working hard at school or on the job, and a multitude of other behaviors are not usually reinforced according to a fixed schedule; our behaviors may be successful two or three times in a row, then not get reinforced the next several times, and so on.

The effects of schedules of reinforcement in our lives are not as neat and predictable as the effects seen in Skinner boxes. There are more complicating factors operating in real life (consider, for example, the many possible variations in reinforcers, in delays between responses and reinforcement, and in degrees of deprivation, each of which can affect response rates). However, that doesn't negate the importance of such schedules in controlling our behaviors. It simply makes it much more difficult to specify exactly what is going on.

We have touched on only some of the possible patterns of reinforcement that can operate. Skinner and a colleague, C. B. Ferster, published a book titled *Schedules of Reinforcement* (Ferster & Skinner, 1957) in which they present the details of intermittent schedules on the basis of years of research. Two of the more complicated arrangements are *multiple schedules* (two or more schedules alternating randomly) and *concurrent schedules* (two or more independent schedules operating at the same time). There is much to consider regarding schedules of reinforcement. They increase the possibility of applying Skinner's psychology to complex human situations.

As a final example in this section, let's consider how different reinforcement schedules might affect sexual activity. Suppose that you are on a *variable-ratio schedule*. In other words, there is always the chance that the next approach to your lover will be reinforced with sexual activity. Isn't it likely that your approaches will be much more frequent and constant than if a pattern has been established by which your sexual advances are reinforced only after a week-long interval has passed? This latter schedule is a *fixed-interval schedule* and would very likely result in long pauses followed by increased seductive approaches around the end of the week.

Chaining

Chaining helps explain smooth sequences of behavior. Sometimes it is difficult to understand how the reinforcement of specific responses can lead to activities such as playing the piano, walking to a restaurant through a maze of city streets, telling a long story, or going through the process of getting ready for school or work in the morning. In Skinner's view, these complex behavior patterns are made up of separate responses joined together in chains. Each response in a chain generates consequences that affect the next response. For example, a piano player's behavior is reinforced when he or she strikes the correct chord. Additionally, however, that chord provides the stimulus for the striking of the next chord, and so on, until the entire piece of music has been played.

The critical factor in chains of behavior is that *discriminative stimuli* can function as *conditioned reinforcers*. Discriminative stimuli indicate that a particular type of behavior, if emitted, is likely to be reinforced. Each response in a chain produces consequences that serve as discriminative stimuli for the next response and that also reinforce the response just made. For example, walking into the kitchen puts one near the refrigerator; this not only may serve as the discriminative stimulus for opening its door but also may reinforce the response of "walking into the kitchen" (assuming that one is hungry). Each behavioral consequence in a chain can be analyzed in this way to show that it functions as *both* a discriminative stimulus and a conditioned reinforcer.

The final reinforcing event that maintains a chain of behavior may involve a primary reinforcer (for example, food). The food-deprived person gets *primary* reinforcement from eating and digesting food, but generally there are many responses that precede the actual act of eating. These responses are reinforced by conditioned reinforcers. Opening the refrigerator door is reinforced by the sight of food, reaching for the food is reinforced by holding the food, putting the food in the oven is reinforced by the smell of it cooking, and so on, until the food is finally eaten (primary reinforcement). The sight of food, the feel of food, and the smell of cooking are all conditioned reinforcers; each is also a discriminative stimulus for the response that follows it in the chain of behavior. They have acquired their reinforcing characteristics by being associated with the primary reinforcement derived from eating.

Typical non-Skinnerian explanations of sequences of behavior usually involve a lot of "decisions." To get something to eat, to go to bed, to visit a friend, to go to the movies, and so on are commonly thought to be the results of conscious and deliberate choices. Skinner's explanation removes decision making and free choice as causes of behavior and focuses on the effects of stimuli and consequences.

Contingencies of Survival and Contingencies of Reinforcement

At this point it should be clear that Skinner's primary focus was on relationships between environmental conditions and behavior, both past and present. As mentioned earlier, he used the phrase "contingencies of survival" to refer to the process of selection that results in the genetic endowment of the species (he also used the phrase "contingencies of natural selection"). Survival is contingent, or dependent, on certain behaviors under certain environmental conditions. Species members that emit these behaviors are more likely to survive and produce offspring, thereby passing on their genetic characteristics, including behavioral tendencies (behaviors that have their origins in the history of a species are "phylogenic" behaviors).

Regarding Skinner's psychology, a critical part of our genetic makeup is that our behaviors are susceptible to their consequences, including the consequences of reinforcement. This makes operant conditioning possible and means that our behaviors are affected greatly by the environmental conditions that occur during our lifetimes. Skinner used the phrase "contingencies of reinforcement" to refer to these conditions and the behaviors involved (behaviors that have their origins in the lifetime of an individual are "ontogenic" behaviors). He suggested that although a part of human behavior can be traced "to natural selection and the evolution of the species [that is, to contingencies of survival] . . . the greater part of human behavior must be traced to contingencies of reinforcement, especially to the very complex social contingencies we call cultures" (Skinner, 1989, p. 24). He defined culture as "the contingencies of social reinforcement maintained by a group" (Skinner, 1987a, p. 74).

Specifically, contingencies of reinforcement are the interrelationships among (1) the conditions under which the behavior occurs, (2) the behavior itself, and (3) the consequences of the behavior (these consequences are another aspect of the environmental conditions). To put it even more simply, stimuli, responses, and reinforcers are interrelated. Consider an example given earlier, of a pigeon that was conditioned to peck a red spot. The contingencies of reinforcement that produced this behavior included the interrelationships among certain conditions or stimuli (especially the red spot that became a discriminative stimulus), the behavior itself (pecking), and reinforcing consequences (the delivery of food); stated succinctly, "pecking the red spot brings food."

The experimental analysis of behavior that Skinner practiced and advocated consisted essentially of arranging various contingencies of reinforcement and observing their effects. This is how he derived the basic concepts that have been discussed in this chapter. Though the majority of his work was done with rats and pigeons, he believed that the same kind of experimental analysis was appropriate and necessary at the human level.

The concept of contingencies of reinforcement is at the heart of Skinner's psychology. He believed that the most successful interpretations of human behavior result from studying the interrelations between the environment and behavior. In addition, the concept leads to the possibility of controlling behavior when the variables discovered are manipulable. Skinner suggested that problems in education, psychotherapy, business, government, daily life, and other areas can be approached most effectively if the problem behaviors themselves, the surrounding conditions, and the consequences of the behaviors can be specified clearly. Once specified, it may be possible to change the contingencies of reinforcement to bring about better behaviors (this work constitutes the field of "applied behavior analysis"). This has been done in many cases, often with good results reported.

An example of arranging contingencies of reinforcement to produce better behaviors is an experiment carried out at a training school for delinquent boys (Skinner, 1969a, pp. 21–22). Boys could earn points by performing certain tasks (working in the kitchen or doing janitorial work) and, more importantly, by studying and learning. The points could then be exchanged for certain foods, a TV set, trips away from the school, a private room, and so on. The general results were that the boys performed useful services, improved their interpersonal relationships, discovered that they could learn, and reported heightened morale. An important aspect of the arrangement of contingencies was that aversive control was minimized. Though not *all* behavioral problems were solved (it is difficult or impossible to control *all* of the important variables in such situations), there were significant improvements.

Skinner's concept of managing contingencies of reinforcement has been used in a variety of settings. To give another example, an approach called "management by consequences" has been developed to help managers in business and industry improve the performance of their employees (Brown, 1982). This approach focuses on the three sets of variables that Skinner proposed. Managers are taught to look closely at work performance in terms of the specific behaviors involved, the conditions (or "antecedents") preceding the behaviors, and the consequences of the behaviors. In the process, they learn to focus on the interrelationships between the environment and behavior and to avoid the common, though nonconstructive, practice of labeling poor-performing employees as lazy, unmotivated, undisciplined, and so on (in other words, the managers learn to look for external, rather than internal, causes for behavior). They also are taught how to change the important variables to bring about better performance (for example, removing aversive stimuli that cause absences or aggressive behavior, making certain that good performance is reinforced quickly, and extinguishing undesirable behavior). This approach has been taught to managers in a number of companies.

To briefly review the major points in this section, Skinner saw the causes of behavior both in the environmental history of the species and in the environmental histories of individuals. The former affects our genetic endowment (which provides certain behavioral characteristics) through contingencies of survival; the latter affects each individual's behavior through the contingencies of reinforcement that prevail during the person's lifetime. (It should be noted that sometimes it is very difficult to determine whether behaviors result from genetic factors or from personal reinforcement histories; these influences can intermingle in complex ways.) For purposes of interpreting and controlling behavior, Skinner emphasized the analysis and manipulation of stimuli, responses, and consequences, which constitute contingencies of reinforcement; these contingencies are relatively accessible when compared to contingencies of survival.

Recently, in psychology and related fields, there has been a resurgence of interest in genetic influences on human behavior. Some of Skinner's critics believe that his approach is threatened by findings that suggest stronger genetic influences than previously suspected. As should be clear from this section, this is a misunderstanding of his views. He gave explicit recognition to genetic endowment as an influence on behavior by referring to contingencies of survival. The *extent* to which genes may affect behavior is a matter to be investigated. Part of the investigation involves analyzing contingencies of reinforcement (the experimental analysis of behavior) and attempting to control behavior by manipulating the accessible variables (applied behavior analysis). This process provides information about the malleability of behavior; the more malleable, the stronger the case for the influence of nurture, rather than nature.

Another way of looking at the relative importance of genes and the environment in determining behavior is that "the genes are all finished once you're born. . . . They're set for life" (Lipsitt, 1990, p. 13). This refers to the fact that genes are a given, even though the actual effects that they will have on behavior are not known at birth. "Whether those genes will have the opportunity to play themselves out, and *how,* depends largely on environmental permissions" (Lipsitt, 1990, p. 13). Though Skinner would have substituted "contingencies of reinforcement" for "environmental permissions," he likely would have agreed with these statements.

Verbal Behavior

For most of his life, Skinner was interested in verbal behavior. Even as a boy he noted certain speech patterns, including his high school principal's regular digressions from the main topic being discussed. Much of his later systematic work is covered in his 1957 book, *Verbal Behavior.* An interesting, though much more limited, presentation is Chapter 6 in *About Behaviorism* (Skinner, 1974, pp. 88–101). Many of his ideas in this area are far too complex and detailed to present here; what follows is a very brief overview, including several of his major points.

According to Skinner (1983b), evolutionary changes in the vocal musculature of the human species allowed operant conditioning to result in language and "the rapid evolution of cultural practices, including 'rational thought' " (p. 85). In his view, language is not a tool for expressing ideas, feelings, needs, desires, or other things in the mind of the speaker: "A much more productive view is that verbal behavior is behavior" (Skinner, 1974, p. 88). As such, it is shaped by the verbal community to which the person belongs; that is, sounds of speech are emitted and have consequences (for example, reinforcement by others) similar to other bits of behavior that occur. Thereby, the complex patterns of speech that we refer to as "language" are shaped.

As with other types of behavior, contingencies of reinforcement are important. Skinner stated this explicitly: ". . . the child's verbal behavior evolves under the selective action of contingencies of reinforcement" (Skinner, 1974, p. 99). The contingencies that shape verbal behavior vary from "indulgent" to "demanding." His example of the former is when parents respond to their child's crude approximations to standard forms of language; his example of the latter is the teaching of diction. In order to interpret the development of verbal behavior, we need to know "the conditions under which it was acquired. What speech has the child heard? Under what circumstances has he heard it? What effects has he achieved when he has uttered similar responses?" (Skinner, 1974, p. 100). Skinner believed that answers to these kinds of questions are required for an adequate analysis of verbal behavior. Even "creative" uses of language, he felt, could be analyzed by acquiring adequate information about contingencies of reinforcement (the verbal behavior itself, the surrounding circumstances, and the reinforcing consequences).

Skinner referred to his interpretation of verbal behavior, and other behaviors as well, as a "functional analysis." He attempted to identify the "external variables of which behavior is a function" (Skinner, 1953, p. 35). In other words, the question is: "What are the relationships between external variables (such as the presence of certain stimuli or the occurrence of certain consequences) and verbal behavior?" If changes in external variables are related to changes in verbal behavior, a "functional relationship" is demonstrated and the behavior is considered to be a "function" of the external variables that produced change.

Skinner identified certain verbal operants, including *mands* and *tacts,* that have characteristic consequences and become part of the person's verbal repertoire. *Mands* occur under conditions of deprivation or aversive stimulation and basically take the form of commands or demands. They are unusual, according to Skinner, in that they *specify* their reinforcing consequences. Once sufficient conditioning has occurred, a person who has not had anything to drink for hours may say "Give me a drink of water," or someone who is being shouted at may say "Stop shouting." The former is reinforced if water is received, and the latter is reinforced if the shouting stops. Mands in simple forms are conditioned early in the development of a child's verbal behavior.

Tacts simply name objects or events, or properties of objects or events. Skinner (1957) indicated that this type of verbal operant is strengthened when "in the presence of the object or event a response of that form is characteristically reinforced in a given verbal community" (p. 82). For example, in the presence of a sunny day and another person, the speaker may say "It's a sunny day." The sunny day is the discriminative stimulus, and the reinforcer is likely to be some response of the other person, such as a nod of the head or the reply "It certainly is." Whereas mands specify particular reinforcers, a variety of reinforcers will do for tacts: when a child says "That's a cat" in the presence of a cat, the parent may applaud or hug the child or say "Yes, a cat!"

While the practices of the verbal community determine how a person speaks, the verbal behavior that develops can then be emitted at almost any time, without environmental support. A very important fact is that the speaker "becomes a listener and may richly reinforce his own behavior" (Skinner, 1974, p. 90); in part, "thinking" consists of our continuous reactions to, and revisions of, our own verbal behavior.

As indicated earlier, Skinner's view of verbal behavior is complex and detailed; in this section, only the surface has been scratched. It should be noted, however, that there are severe critics of his interpretations. One argument is that there are strong innate factors affecting the development of language abilities and that we are inherently prepared to learn language (see Klein, 1987, pp. 345–348, for a brief comparison of Skinner's view with that of linguist Noam Chomsky, a well-known critic of Skinner).* Of course, *both* nature and nurture may affect verbal behavior. As Klein (1987) indicates: "A contemporary view suggests that both preparedness and the use of conditioning influence language; humans may be prepared to learn language, but they must also discover that language can be used to obtain nonsocial and social rewards" (p. 353). Skinner's functional analysis relates to Klein's latter point by suggesting the effects that external variables have on verbal behavior.

---

*For example, see Chomsky (1959), listed among the Annotated References. Skinner believed his work was misunderstood by Chomsky and, therefore, that Chomsky's criticisms lacked validity (Skinner, 1983b, pp. 153–155).

In this chapter, many of Skinner's basic concepts were discussed. Some of the most important points were that (1) operant behavior can be strengthened through positive or negative reinforcement; (2) reinforcers can be either primary or conditioned; (3) some behaviors are "superstitious"—that is, there is only an accidental connection between them and reinforcement; (4) operant behaviors that are not reinforced tend to extinguish; (5) punishment typically suppresses behavior but doesn't necessarily do so permanently; (6) responses that are reinforced in particular situations tend to generalize to similar situations, but discrimination develops if reinforcement occurs only in particular situations and not in others; (7) complex behaviors are shaped through the differential reinforcement of closer and closer approximations to the final behaviors; (8) different schedules of reinforcement yield different response rates, patterns of responding, and resistances to extinction; (9) ongoing sequences of behavior can be considered as "chains" in which discriminative stimuli also serve as conditioned reinforcers; (10) contingencies of survival lead to the genetic endowment of the species, whereas contingencies of reinforcement lead to the behaviors acquired by individuals during their lifetimes; and (11) verbal behavior, like other behaviors, can be subjected to a "functional analysis" in which the relationships between external variables and verbal behavior are examined.

THREE

Sources of Controversy

SKINNER AROUSED more than his share of controversy, and it continues. He may be the *most* controversial figure in the history of psychology, although Sigmund Freud, and perhaps John B. Watson (the founder of behaviorism), also merit consideration. Though the major reasons why Skinner is so disputed are somewhat intertwined, they can be discussed separately:

1. Skinner's radical determinism contradicts the American ideal of self-determination. It opposes concepts of free choice, personal responsibility, and rugged individualism. Also, it follows that, if our behavior is fully determined by past and present conditions, we can't "take credit" for our accomplishments.

2. He emphasized that, by controlling the environment, we can control behavior, and he advocated that we should do this to improve our society and our lives. This disturbs those who don't like the connotations of the word "control" or the implications of "being controlled."

3. He originally based his suggestions for improving human behavior on findings from research with lower animals. There are critics who feel that such findings are not relevant to human activities and/or that it is insulting to apply them to humans.

4. His behavioral concepts often have been interpreted simplistically. This has resulted in criticism from those who feel that he either ignored or negated the richness of human life.

Each of these four sources of controversy will now be discussed in more detail.

The American Ideal of Self-Determination versus Radical Determinism

Skinner isn't often taken lightly. He generally excites a definite reaction, sometimes positive but often negative. He challenged certain established and cherished ways of thinking about ourselves, especially our emphasis on individual free choice and personal responsibility. Our economic, political, legal, and other social systems are influenced strongly by the view that each person is self-determining.

Skinner's approach conflicts with this view. He can be considered a radical determinist: an individual's *genetic endowment, past history of personal experiences,* and *present environmental conditions* explain his or her behavior ("contingencies of survival" account for genetic endowment, and "contingencies of reinforcement" apply to the latter two factors). Essentially, all three of these factors are environmental, because even genetic endowment is determined by the influence of the environment on our evolutionary ancestors. This emphasis on environmental determinants of behavior refutes the American ideal of the strong, independent person who is self-determining, an individual who makes free choices and takes personal responsibility for "making something" of himself or herself. Skinner's determinism is a proposition, about which he wrote: "We cannot prove, of course, that human behavior as a whole is fully determined, but the proposition becomes more plausible as facts accumulate . . ." (Skinner, 1974, p. 189).

Probably most of us would agree that *in fact* many aspects of our society do not operate according to individual free choice and responsibility, and that we often cannot really determine what our accomplishments will be. For example, our competitive economic system provides fair competition for only a minority. The rest do not have the means to compete effectively since they lack the necessary skills, material support, and/or appropriate opportunities. In the political realm, positions are held by those who supposedly have the "will and determination" to seek and win public office, but in reality it often seems that money, prestige, and family influence are the determinants. Our legal system claims to administer justice fairly and makes the general assumption that each individual is responsible for his or her own behavior. But would anyone argue that our legal institutions actually are equitable to rich and poor, White and Black, powerful and powerless? Furthermore, most people would grant that not all persons, even when they are sane, are equally responsible for their criminal acts. Ignorance, extreme deprivation, and harshness of childhood experiences, as well as other factors, are often considered to be extenuating circumstances, even though the courts may not consistently take these factors into account.

The points to be made are these: The concepts of individual responsibility and self-determination are well ingrained in American society and continue to be held close to our hearts, despite the fact that our institutions (and many of our lives) are riddled with examples that deny freedom and equal opportunity for each person. Most of us have been taught that we are the masters of our own fates, at least to some degree. However, we've also learned that we must accept and live with certain disadvantages and that we shouldn't expect to get everything we want. In other words, "Yes, you are what you make of yourself through your own willpower, personal fortitude, ingenuity, and so on," *but* (and this is the catch) "No, you will not necessarily have the same opportunities and advantages as others, and therefore you shouldn't expect to make out as well as you might like to." These two somewhat contradictory teachings explain how we are able to maintain a vital belief in individual freedom of choice and determination, although the evidence around us reveals many limits and restrictions on what most of us accomplish.

Enter B. F. Skinner, who maintained that it is the environment (interpreted broadly to include all the social and physical conditions—past, present, and future—of which we are a part) that determines what we are and what we will become (remember, he accounted for genetic inheritance by referring to the environments that existed during evolutionary history). At first glance this doesn't seem radical. The reaction might be: "Did he say that we are affected by the environment? That makes sense. Obviously the conditions around us have some effect on us. I can accept that without any problem." Eventually, however, it becomes clear that he said that environmental factors determine our behavior in such a way that "free will" and "individual choice" play no causal role.

The next reaction is apt to be a bit different from the first: "Now wait just a minute. Did I get that right? Our behavior is *completely* determined by conditions that have nothing to do with free thought or choice? That's ridiculous! I know some things are out of my control and that I don't get everything I want, but most of what I feel and do depends on *me*. If I don't feel like doing something, I don't do it. If I do decide to do something, I do it. *I* control things most of the time. Skinner went way too far in what he said, and I don't buy it."

It's the extent to which Skinner said we are influenced by the environment that causes controversy. He carried this assumption to a point where many people "don't buy it." As mentioned before, it violates what we have learned as members of a "free society" and goes against traditional concepts such as strong individualism, free choice, "being one's own person," and "making it" through personal drive and ingenuity. If your environment is primarily responsible for your success and determines your effectiveness, how can you be proud of your accomplishments? Where is the satisfaction if you don't do it your own? These types of questions indicate the way people feel when they are asked to give up their ideas of self-determination. Though they are willing to agree that *sometimes* external factors and "luck" influence their fates, Skinner's more extreme position makes them feel that the very meaning of life is being challenged. Is it any wonder that Skinner stirs them up?

Most of us are willing to admit that we have had help in our achievements. Writers place acknowledgments at the front of their books, scientists thank colleagues and research-funding agencies, students express gratitude to their teachers, and athletes point out the debt they owe to their coaches. However, it is exceptional when a person relinquishes all credit for his or her good performance. More typically, we do take a large part of the credit ourselves (though to do so publicly in a blatant way is frowned on). Also, we usually expect to be admired for the "strong personal qualities" that bring us success, especially when the external influences on our behaviors are subtle; if the external influences are obvious, we are less likely to take credit.

The Skinnerian scheme of things doesn't allow for individual credit taking in the usual sense. An individual is born with a given genetic makeup; certainly we deserve no credit for any unique hereditary qualities that we may have, since these qualities are bestowed in a way that is completely outside our control. After birth, the social and physical environments exert their influences on us. Skinner suggested that these conditions also are not chosen or decided on by us; they simply exist and have effects. Therefore we can take no greater credit for what we become after being born than we can for what we were at birth. In neither case do we freely choose or decide what conditions will affect us or what we will become. Skinner believed that this applied to him, as well as to the rest of us; he wrote: "So far as I know, my behavior at any given moment has been nothing more than the product of my genetic endowment, my personal history, and the current setting" (Skinner, 1983c, p. 25).

This doesn't mean, though, that we aren't "individualistic," if that term can be changed somewhat from its usual meaning, which implies a kind of self-determined, freely chosen set of personal qualities. According to Skinner, each of us is unique (different from every other person) but not because we have chosen or decided to be so. Rather, our individualities spring from two facts: our genetic structures differ (except in the case of identical twins), *and* each of us is exposed to different experiences. It would be impossible for two persons (even identical twins) to have precisely the same experiences in every detail. These variations contribute to producing individuals who differ from one another. An important point here is that dramatic differences in experiences are not necessary to produce different "personalities." Even subtle, perhaps almost unnoticeable, differences can have an effect.

It isn't hard to accept this type of reasoning, to a point. The idea that hereditary factors and early life experiences are outside of individual control seems very reasonable. But, once again, Skinner carried things beyond what is reasonable to many people by suggesting that the influence of environmental factors does not diminish as we grow older. He did suggest that we may become increasingly able to deal effectively with our environmental conditions because of our expanding behavior repertoires. In other words, with maturity we usually are capable of making a greater variety of responses, especially if a variety of constructive and adaptive behaviors have been reinforced, and this gives us a certain amount of "independence." It is not an independence based on free choice and autonomy, however. Rather, it is based on the increased quantity and types of responses we can make, and this depends on our physiological development and experiences.

For Skinner, there is no developing ego or self that eventually is able to take over and give deliberate, conscious, rational direction to our lives. In other words, the individual is not able, even with maturity, to wrestle control away from external factors and become removed from environmental control. We remain, in Skinner's eyes, under the influence of our environments from birth to death. This is a foreign and irritating opinion to many people. Who wants to believe that we can't rise above surrounding circumstances and be free and autonomous? This is a cherished hope and belief that Skinnerian psychology tampers with, and those who hold it get impatient, annoyed, or angry when it is challenged.

The Concept of Control

Tied closely to the strict determinism of Skinner's approach is his re-peated use of the term "control." This is another major cause of the controversy that churns around Skinner's ideas. Control is important in Skinnerian psychology in various ways, but the basic assumption is that environmental conditions control (that is, either maintain or change) behavior in systematic ways. This assumption goes back to Skinner's early work with animals in the laboratories at Harvard University and remained with him through his many years as a researcher, teacher, lecturer, and writer. It is a concept with much supporting evidence. The laboratory studies of Skinner and others have shown time and again that, if conditions are set in certain ways, the behavior of rats, pigeons, and other lower animals can be predicted with a great deal of precision. For example, if a food-deprived rat receives a food pellet (a reinforcer) whenever it presses the lever in a Skinner box, it will soon press the lever repeatedly whenever it has been deprived of food. Also, the rate at which the rat works can be changed by altering the number of presses required to receive reinforcers. These are very simple examples. Laboratory studies have revealed many more complex relationships between environmental manipulations and behavioral outcomes. Also, it is very important to realize that research on environmental effects is not limited to animal studies. Humans have been studied under various environmental conditions, and it has been shown that we, too, are susceptible to their influence and often respond predictably.

The concept of control, then, became central in Skinner's thinking at an early stage of his work as a psychologist. Though at first concentrating on the ways in which he could set conditions in order to get reliable, predictable behaviors from lower animals, he eventually extended his views to include the control of human behavior. According to Skinner, humans also are subject to the controlling influences of environmental factors, and therefore social conditions can be set up in ways that will yield predictable behavioral outcomes. Frequently he has sug-gested that we should take seriously the idea of cultural design and plan our social institutions so that people will be productive, secure, creative, healthy, and happy. He felt that too often these things are left to chance.

As in the case of radical determinism, discussed previously, a moderate version of Skinner's suggestions would arouse little disagreement. Who would deny that we should look carefully at our society and try to make it better through constructive changes? It is the seemingly extreme nature of the proposal that provokes people, and this extremism becomes embodied in the word *control*. Using the term repeatedly, Skinner did more than simply consider desirable changes in social conditions and institutions—he advocated that we accept the unalterable fact that we *are* controlled and that we then move ahead and plan the environment in such a way that society runs smoothly and beneficially. Few of us want to be convinced that we actually are controlled by forces outside ourselves, but Skinner continually rubs our faces in that assumption. "Freedom" is what most persons want to hear about, not "control."

Additional aspects of the control issue also get people upset. *Who* is to do the controlling and to what ends? Skinner himself was not always clear in his responses to these questions but indicated that persons already in positions to exert control could be more effective if they knew and used his behavioral concepts. These persons are parents, teachers, supervisors, and others in charge of making or implementing decisions. However, a common fear among Skinner's critics is that the power to control will become invested in some dictatorial group, who will then apply behavior-control procedures for their own ends. Sometimes Skinner is accused of having provided information that can be abused by power-hungry individuals.

Another question is: how could we decide which behaviors to control? Skinner suggested that we could agree on certain desirable goals, such as happiness, productivity, and creativity. We could then go ahead and systematically experiment with techniques for controlling the environmental conditions that produce these outcomes. Though this seems like a simple proposal, it isn't always seen in that light. Skinner has been criticized for being too general and vague. Wouldn't there be conflict about the specifics of happiness, productivity, creativity, and so on?

Generalizations from Animals to Humans

The origin of Skinner's concepts of behavior control—laboratory studies of rats and pigeons—is another point that makes his ideas controversial. Even though there have been successful applications of Skinnerian concepts at the human level, their original source is not forgotten and continues to be criticized and resented. Criticism often centers around the idea that the complexity of humans puts them into an entirely different category from lower animals, and therefore any observed similarities in behavior are more apparent than real. The argument is made that, even though certain common relationships may be observed between environmental manipulations and behavioral outcomes in both animals and humans, the dynamics differ. For example, the behaviors of both rats and humans tend to increase in frequency when certain consequences occur, but is the reason the same? Perhaps humans "figure out" what is going on by using rational thought processes and then "decide" to behave as they do in order to get reinforced. With rats the process may be more "mechanical"—that is, determined by the neurophysiological makeup of the organism with no conscious or rational self-determination taking place.

There also are those who just plain resent likening humans to animals. They feel that to listen to ideas that grew out of animal research is to degrade the human condition. They don't want to consider a psychology that had such lowly beginnings, and they feel that behavioral concepts and procedures drawn from studies of rats and pigeons are unfit for humankind. They are offended by Skinner's attempts to look at our behavior in a light similar to that in which he observed his laboratory animals.

Simple Behavioral Analysis

Still another aspect of Skinnerian psychology arouses controversy: its apparent simplicity, which sometimes is translated as "oversimplification." The following comments are typical: "Maybe what Skinner said is correct as far as it goes, but it certainly doesn't apply to the full complexity of human behavior. His system is absurdly oversimplified. He didn't even begin to capture the richness of human life." The assumption frequently made is that Skinner didn't deal with human feelings and thoughts and that he had nothing to say about complex behaviors such as those displayed in creative activities. Even persons who know that he did discuss these matters often are not satisfied with his explanations. In either case, whether it is believed that Skinner avoided such issues or that his formulations are inadequate, there is cause for strong reactions. He has been accused of pushing a system that ignores the full meaning of being human.*

In the next chapter, the sources of controversy indicated here are discussed again, for the purpose of pointing out misunderstandings that sometimes intensify the criticisms that are made of Skinner's approach. In addition, several other topics that are especially likely to cause misunderstandings are covered.

---

*The sources of controversy covered in this chapter have had general and widespread effects. For coverage of more specific controversial issues of special concern to those in psychology and related fields, see Modgil and Modgil (1987) and Proctor and Weeks (1990), listed among the Annotated References.

FOUR

Common Misunderstandings

AT LEAST IN PART, the controversy that Skinner generates is due to misunderstandings of what he said. The reasons for these misunderstandings involve both Skinner and his audience. On the one hand, some of his writings are difficult to grasp in detail. On the other hand, not all of Skinner's critics read his works with sufficient care.

In Chapter Three, four major reasons were given for the controversy over Skinner's ideas. Those reasons gain even more power to arouse disputes if misunderstandings exist. Let's look briefly at each of them again to try to clarify Skinner's actual positions. The goal is not to explain away all sources of controversy, but rather to clear away confusion and possible misinterpretations. There will continue to be those who have real disagreements with Skinner; opposition based on a thorough understanding of what he said can be stimulating and productive.

Self-Determination versus Radical Determinism

It is quite true that Skinner denied that our behaviors are self-determined by our inner states of mind or emotion; he explained behavior by pointing to genetic inheritance and individual experiences with surrounding social and physical environments. In his view, then, we are not self-determining in the usual sense of that phrase. Also, certain traditional American ideals, such as personal responsibility and rugged individualism, have little place in his scheme of things. Skinner believed that our devotion to such ideals has hindered progress toward developing a society in which citizens are more productive, creative, secure, and happy. He suggested that we rely too heavily on assumed inner qualities (personal motivation, drive, willpower, fortitude, and so on) for the determination of success. We talk about freedom and opportunity for all, hoping to encourage individual efforts and achievements, but, in Skinner's opinion, this is a relatively ineffective way to improve life and to ensure the continued survival of a strong society. It leaves too much to chance. Too many persons get passed by and spend their lives in apathy or frustration, not being able to develop their potential, missing opportunities to improve themselves, and failing to contribute to society.

Skinner believed that it would be far more effective to use available information about the effects of environmental conditions on behavior, information that has come from studies of both animals and humans. He suggested that, by doing this (that is, by engaging in behavioral engineering), environments can be developed that will benefit both individuals and society. In brief, Skinner advocated that we give up our reverence for self-determination, face the facts, and turn toward environmental planning, since it is the environment that can be counted on to influence behavior.

A major misunderstanding regarding these issues is the common belief that Skinner's proposals are totally (or almost totally) opposed to our most cherished ideals. Though he did challenge self-determination by denying that we freely and autonomously decide or choose how we are going to behave, he strongly supported other important traditional beliefs: the ideals of maximizing each person's potential, creating more happiness and satisfaction, and having a strong and effective society. He wanted his principles to be used to accomplish these goals.

Another misunderstanding sometimes arises out of Skinner's attack on the concept of personal responsibility (which is related closely to self-determination). He reasoned that, since we all are products of genetic and environmental factors, it isn't reasonable to hold individuals responsible for their behaviors. This worries those who feel that widespread acceptance of Skinner's ideas would bring on a rash of irresponsible and criminal behaviors by people who would say: "I'm not responsible for what I do. Circumstances are at fault. Don't blame me." Two points need to be made here. First, this type of excuse already is used by many delinquents, criminals, and others who behave in antisocial ways. Skinner provided no new excuse for them. Second, our present system of placing personal responsibility on people is not notably successful. We have plenty of irresponsible and criminal behavior in our society. Maybe such behaviors could be reduced by relying less on individual responsibility and more on the careful analysis and restructuring of environmental conditions.

Skinner pointed out that maximum study and use of constructive environmental changes are delayed by clinging to the notion of personal responsibility (and this was his main reason for objecting to it). Of course, we already accept to some extent the fact that environmental conditions affect behavior, and various social programs are designed to reduce delinquent, criminal, and other undesirable activities. However, by Skinner's standards these often are halfhearted attempts based on faulty behavioral concepts or procedures. According to him, a more consistent, rigorous, and informed effort is needed.

There also is misunderstanding regarding the term "self-determination." Actually, the term can be used in Skinnerian psychology if its meaning is altered somewhat. In fact, as will be discussed later in this chapter, Skinner sometimes used a closely related term, "self-control." As noted repeatedly, Skinner's ideas are opposed to traditional connotations of "self-determination." But, in a different sense, people *do* influence their environments, which in turn influence them. In other words, we aren't simply passive organisms. Almost all of Skinner's behavioral concepts are based on the fact that we are active and responsive. As we behave, we affect the social and physical worlds around us; we alter our environments. These alterations then affect us. There is an interaction between us and our environments. *Ultimately, it is the environment that has control,* but our behaviors (because they act to change the environment) play a role in the types of influence that the environment has. This issue will be discussed in more detail shortly.

As mentioned previously, in Skinner's radical determinism no room is given to an ego, a self, or any other inner autonomous agent that might direct our behavior. He rejected the idea that such internal agents allow us to make independent and free choices. Accordingly, our choices and decisions are never really free. They always depend on our basic genetic structure and, very importantly, on our exposure to a multitude of environmental conditions. We can never be free from these influences; they are always the final determinants of our behavior.

This has been criticized as an unacceptable, or even ridiculous, philosophy. If Skinner were correct, wouldn't it be completely depressing to live out one's life? Wouldn't everything be so predictable that the anticipation and excitement of life would be gone? Again, we are moving into an area where misunderstandings are likely to occur. As Skinner suggested, to say that we live completely *determined* lives doesn't lead to the conclusion that we live completely *predictable* lives. In the first place, it is impossible to be absolutely certain about all of the genetic characteristics of a person. Though these genetic characteristics exist and influence behavior, they are not completely knowable to the person or to others. In other words, neither we nor others can be certain what the effects of our genes will be.

The same can be said about the environment. Even when a great deal is known about one's environment, it isn't possible to know everything. Subtle environmental conditions can affect behavior, so it isn't possible (with presently existing techniques) to make *completely* accurate predictions about behavioral outcomes. Also, various unique interactions between genetic and environmental factors can occur, causing other unpredictable outcomes. Taking all these considerations into account, one can agree with Skinner's radical determinism and still look forward to a life that is unpredictable and exciting.

There might appear to be a contradiction here of earlier statements about the possibilities of using behavioral engineering. Skinner advocated the planning of environmental conditions so that behaviors beneficial to individuals and to society will be developed and maintained. But can this occur if behavior is as unpredictable as has just been suggested? The answer to this is that predictability isn't an all-or-nothing affair. By carefully controlling certain environmental conditions, the likelihood of getting certain desired behavioral outcomes is increased significantly. However, some unpredictability always will exist, even in a society carefully controlled along Skinnerian lines. It is likely that certain genetic and environmental factors, and their effects on behavior, will continue to remain unknown. This doesn't invalidate Skinner's deterministic view; it simply means that some of the multitude of factors that affect our behaviors will remain uncontrolled and therefore some behaviors will not be completely predictable.

Yet another misunderstanding that derives from Skinner's strict determinism is the implication that we are *completely* at the whim of either fate or the controlling influences of others. Critics have pointed to the fatalism that they feel is inherent in his psychology. How can anything have any meaning in a system based on such an assumption? Aren't we simply pawns in a game if radical determinism is true? In response to such questions, it must be pointed out that, according to Skinner, each of us does have an effect on the social and physical environments with which we have contact. They are altered by each of us. The individual does count, in the sense that each person's behaviors are a real part of the real world and therefore influence that world.

Though these statements might appear to indicate some backsliding from the position of strict determinism, they are not really inconsistent with Skinner's view. Because of genetic endowment, past experiences, and present circumstances, we *will* behave in certain ways (in other words, our behavior *is* determined). The behaviors that we emit, however, change the environment in some way—that is, produce consequences of some sort. These consequences in turn affect our behaviors, and so on. According to Skinner, each of us is a vital link, *a unique locus of events,* in this process. Therefore our behaviors *are* meaningful in that they produce environmental changes that affect us. To refer back to an earlier point, though we are not self-determining in the traditional sense of having free choice about how we behave, we can be considered self-determining in the Skinnerian sense that our actions have outcomes that influence our future behaviors. We are not simply pawns in a game, since the behavior of each individual, based on his or her own particular hereditary and experiential factors, is unique.

This gets us back to the important issue of credit taking, discussed in Chapter Three. Does the reasoning in the previous paragraph mean that we can take some personal credit for our accomplishments, since these accomplishments are unique and individualistic contributions? However comforting it might be to answer "yes" to this question, in the strict Skinnerian sense the answer is "no." Each of us does make unique and individualistic contributions, but not because of some special inner quality. Rather, these contributions derive from each person's genetic structure, past experiences, and present circumstances—and none of these are conditions for which the person can take credit. We do not, through admirable acts of free and autonomous judgment or choice, determine these factors.

The Concept of Control

One of the most frequent misunderstandings of Skinner's emphasis on control is the assumption that it's a one-way process. The mere mention of controlling environmental factors in order to control human behavior disturbs persons who think in terms of free and independent action. When it is believed additionally that control works solely in a hierarchical fashion, from controller to controllee, it is even more upsetting (perhaps it stirs up ideas of dictatorial control).

However, in situations designed according to Skinner's suggestions, the controller/controllee distinction is minimized; there is no concentration of power in the controller. Let's assume that the controller is a person appointed or selected to establish goals and/or regulate behavior. Though this is a position of influence, Skinner reminds us that (in a well-planned system) those being managed by the controller also have a good deal of power to *countercontrol* (that is, they can directly and significantly influence the controller's behaviors). This countercontrol ensures against the misuse of power by controllers.

Countercontrol can take various forms. Ideally, appropriate behaviors of both controllers and controllees are reinforced. In a Skinnerian society the controllers (for example, teachers, parents, and work supervisors) attempt to control the environment in such a way that clearly stated behavioral outcomes result. In order to get these behavioral outcomes, Skinner suggested that the best methods are those based on the use of positive reinforcement. Some positive reinforcers are material things such as money and food. Other positive reinforcers are more socially based: praise, attention, and so on. Another type of positive reinforcer is simply "being effective." Skinner points out that this seems to be a very basic feature of humans: often our behaviors are reinforced simply by the environmental changes they produce, rather than by some material or social reinforcer.

Clearly, then, controllers have a variety of positive reinforcers with which to control behavior. But how about the controllees? What can they use to countercontrol? Perhaps the most direct means is their performance. If the controllers are doing their jobs properly, the controllees will perform well. Good performance reinforces the controller's behaviors because they have been effective. (Being effective, of course, may lead to other reinforcers for the controller: pay raises, promotions, praise from others, and so on.) On the other hand, poor performance on the part of controllees is likely to extinguish or punish the controller's behaviors and may result in a revision of methods that are causing poor performance.

If the situation deteriorates—for example, if the controller moves to aversive methods such as threats of punishment for poor performance—then other countercontrolling measures may be used by controllees. They may leave the situation (for example, the student may cut classes, the child may run away from home, and the employee may fake illness or quit the job); they may aggress against the controller (for example, talking back to a teacher, parent, or supervisor); they may produce other aversive conditions for the controller (the student may "act up" and disrupt the class, the child may throw temper tantrums, and the employee may use sabotage). Obviously these methods of countercontrol do not allow a smooth-running, effective, and pleasant situation. Therefore, as Skinner repeatedly emphasized, it is important to plan situations so that positive reinforcement occurs without the necessity of aversive controlling and countercontrolling measures. It is interesting to ask: "How many controller/controllee situations in our present society are characterized by mutual positive reinforcement and the absence of aversive conditions?"

Getting back to the main point that launched us into this discussion of methods of countercontrol, it must be emphasized again that countercontrol is a vital part of Skinner's plan. If this is remembered, it helps offset the possible misinterpretation that those being controlled in a Skinnerian society would be powerless victims of manipulations by controllers. Skinner is well aware of the dangers inherent in situations in which people lack the power to countercontrol effectively. In fact, he pointed out that it is instructive to look at five groups of people in our present society who have little countercontrolling influence: the aged, young children, retarded persons, prisoners, and psychotics. They are frequently treated poorly, with a lack of compassion. They generally don't have the means to exert effective countercontrol and therefore have to rely on the intervention of others on their behalf. In a society using Skinner's behavioral concepts, safeguards would be set up to ensure better treatment of these persons. In other words, "compassion" would be ensured through environmental control.

As stated before, the connotations of the word "control" got Skinner into a lot of trouble. It seems opposed to the dignity of human life. But is this a valid assumption, or is it a misunderstanding of what Skinner said? What Skinner typically meant when he recommended "control" is that environmental conditions be altered in order to establish desirable behaviors. The "undignified" aspect of this goes back to issues that were discussed earlier; it challenges traditional assumptions about humans as free, autonomous, and self-determining. However, if better environmental control resulted in more productive, happy, healthy, and creative people, wouldn't that increase our dignity or worth? This partly depends on what is valued most: holding onto traditional concepts of human dignity and freedom *or* attempting to control the environment to improve our behaviors.

One final comment will be made about control, in response to two questions that often are asked: If Skinner's concepts of control are valid, isn't there a danger that they'll be used by malevolent persons to benefit themselves? Isn't Skinner suggesting the means by which such persons can control others for selfish reasons? As Skinner himself admitted, his behavioral concepts and procedures can be misused. There is no absolute, foolproof way of guarding against this possibility, but the same is true of many other types of knowledge. (Skinner used the example of atomic energy, which can be used for good or evil purposes.) However, there are quicker and easier ways for evil persons to get their way; they can and do use threats, physical force, and other aversive methods. Skinner's proposals for controlling behavior advocate the systematic use of positive reinforcement, rather than aversive methods of control.

Generalizations from Animals to Humans

There is no doubt that Skinner's early attempts to discuss human situations and problems, and his suggestions for improvements, were based heavily on findings from his laboratory studies using rats and pigeons as subjects. For example, his novel, *Walden Two,* written in 1945 and published in 1948, was an attempt to apply what he had learned about behavioral control to the construction of a utopian community. He believed that behavioral concepts developed by studying lower animals in carefully designed and controlled experiments might apply at the human level.

Since the publication of *Walden Two,* much additional research has been carried out, using both animal and human subjects. Studies have been done with psychotic, neurotic, retarded, and normal children and adults. Skinner's ideas and procedures have been used effectively by psychologists and others in settings such as schools for delinquents, hospitals and institutions, public schools, colleges and universities, therapists' offices, and family situations. Under various circumstances, delinquent behaviors have been changed; psychotic and retarded persons have been trained to be more self-sufficient; behavioral and learning problems among schoolchildren have been reduced; students have learned more efficiently using teaching machines and programmed instruction; therapists have helped clients change their troublesome and maladaptive behaviors; and parents have been instructed in the use of behavioral procedures for interacting more effectively with their children. The list of places where Skinnerian practices have been applied at the human level could go on and would include businesses, nursing homes, day-care centers, and rehabilitation wards.* So, even though Skinner's own research did not focus on human subjects, his concepts have been widely researched and applied by others working with people.

Considerable evidence now exists that Skinner's behavioral techniques (often referred to as "operant procedures") are effective with humans in a wide variety of situations. No longer can his psychology be considered as applying primarily to rats and pigeons; it has gone far beyond its origins. The phrase "behavior modification" has become common, referring to the application of Skinnerian methods, as well as certain procedures developed by others, to human problems and situations. (Skinner himself preferred the phrase "applied behavior analysis," which refers specifically to the use of operant procedures to improve contingencies of reinforcement).

The criticism that Skinner overgeneralized from simple animal studies to complex human behaviors has never been a very sound one. He had never said that humans and lower animals are just alike; rather, he drew *assumptions* about human behavior from animal research. The mistake would be to say: "We know this about rats and pigeons; therefore we also know this about humans." Skinner's approach was to use findings from animal research to formulate behavioral concepts that can be tested out at the human level. In other words, once it has been found that certain environmental conditions are related to certain behavior patterns among rats or pigeons, the question is: "Do similar relationships between

---

*For a popular article on the spreading use of behavior modification, see Kenneth Goodall, "Shapers at Work," *Psychology Today,* November 1972, pp. 53–63, 132–138. Also, see Alan E. Kazdin, "The Rich Rewards of REWARDS," *Psychology Today,* November 1976, pp. 98–105, 114. Although these articles certainly are not the most recent, they are very easy to read and are informative.

environmental conditions and behavior exist for humans?" Findings from animal studies may *possibly* hold true at the human level. However, it is always a matter of collecting data to verify that they do. In the case of *Walden Two*, it must be remembered that it is a novel and was not written as an *actual* account of the application of Skinner's concepts at the social level. It was an account of the *possibilities* of applying his concepts. As Skinner stated, he was "guessing" when he wrote the book. If written today, because of the widespread use of behavior-modification programs, less guessing would be required.

Though there is little real basis for faulting Skinner on the issue of generalizing from lower animals to humans, there is another criticism concerning overgeneralization that carries more weight. There is a difference between using behavioral procedures effectively in carefully circumscribed settings within mental institutions, school systems, business organizations, and so on, and applying them at the level of society as a whole. In his 1971 book *Beyond Freedom and Dignity,* and in other publications as well, Skinner made bold proposals for changes in our social system, strongly suggesting that the very survival of our society may depend on the adoption of a behavioral-engineering approach. He didn't say simply that behavior modification (or, more specifically, applied behavior analysis) has been used successfully in a wide variety of human situations and that its use should therefore be extended; he went well beyond that, recommending, in essence, that the social structure be revamped along Skinnerian lines.

This proposal has caused heated reactions. Was Skinner justified in making society-wide claims for his approach on the basis of its past and current effectiveness? As indicated, the successes are numerous. Still, these successes derive mainly from behavior-modification programs carried out in situations, and under circumstances, that are quite specific and limited when compared with the extent and complexity of major political, legal, economic, and other social institutions. It is debatable, despite the evidence that has accumulated since the 1950s, that Skinner's behavioral techniques would be effective if applied on a massive scale. Also, too little is known about the possible dangers and drawbacks of society-wide application. Perhaps he was premature in advocating total acceptance of his approach.

In fairness to Skinner, it must be pointed out again that embedded in his behavioral-engineering approach is a safeguard that should help prevent any serious damage to society's fabric from the adoption of his ideas. This safeguard is the experimental method. If a condition is altered, its effects are observed carefully. By observing relationships between environmental manipulations and behavioral outcomes, progress can be monitored and changes can be made if necessary. If this approach is used, the chances of getting way off the track are lessened considerably. Of course, there still are opportunities for human errors such as poor data collection and biased conclusions, but these are present under any system; perhaps they are less likely to occur with a behavioral-engineering approach such as applied behavior analysis, because of its continual emphasis on the need for careful observations. Skinner also suggested that we should think about forming small experimental communities (like Walden Two) in order to test out various behavioral approaches. On a small scale, it would be easier to implement changes and to observe their effects.

Before we go to the next section, a final point will be made. As mentioned in Chapter Three, some critics have said that even though the behaviors of lower animals and humans sometimes seem to be affected similarly by environmental events, the underlying reasons may be different. Rats and pigeons may behave "automatically," without thinking, but humans think and make decisions. For example, if a rat presses a lever again after having received a food pellet for the previous press, this may be simply a mechanical-type response, involving no higher thought processes. However, if a person repeats a response that has just been reinforced, he or she may have "figured out" what's going on and "decided" to behave in the way that will bring a reward.

In reply, it must be admitted that it is very hard to disprove the idea that conscious decisions lie behind most human behaviors. However, if time and again it can be shown that particular environmental events have predictable behavioral outcomes, is there any good reason to assume that human behavior is guided by thought? Thinking may be going on, but is it this thinking or the environmental event that determines the behavior? Two things (thought and some event) are occurring. Which is the actual cause of the behavior? Skinner voted for the environmental event and said that the accompanying thought processes are not influential. In fact, they too are influenced by what is occurring environmentally. (This issue will be taken up again soon, in the section "Feelings and Thoughts.")

Simple Behavioral Analysis

Is Skinner's analysis of human behavior really oversimplified? Certainly there are many critics who claim it is. Again, misunderstandings sometimes are at the root of these claims. One of the popular conceptions (or misconceptions) of Skinnerian psychology is that it simply states the obvious: behaviors can be strengthened by their consequences. One such consequence is *positive reinforcement,* the backbone of Skinner's approach. It may seem to be simple folk wisdom, meaning that we all are likely to do what pays off in money, prestige, attention from others, sexual contacts, or other "rewards" for our efforts. After all, don't salespersons sell to earn commissions, students study for good grades, children "act up" to get the attention of their playmates, and lovers behave romantically to have sexual relations? So what's the big deal about "positive reinforcement"? Why is it anything special? Isn't it just a simple idea, one that we all know works in certain situations?

The apparent simplicity of positive reinforcement is deceptive. Skinner and his colleagues used it to get animals and humans to perform very complex behaviors. For example, during World War II, through appropriate schedules of reinforcement, pigeons were taught in the laboratory to guide missiles (they were never used militarily). A good example at the human level is "programmed instruction. " By reinforcing very simple correct responses at first, then requiring more and more advanced responses for reinforcement, programmed-learning materials lead the student, stepwise, toward the development of complex skills and knowledge. (For adults, simply being informed that they have given the correct answer usually is sufficient reinforcement to keep them working.) Of course, this is what is supposed to occur in most training programs and classrooms. But, as Skinner pointed out, this process often occurs in a relatively inefficient manner; typically the material to be learned is not broken down into sufficiently small units (thereby causing confusion), and the student's behavior is not reinforced in a systematic way. It is important, for example, to provide immediate reinforcement; the student should be given immediate feedback about the correctness of his or her answers. In contrast, students in the typical classroom often do not receive examination results until quite some time has passed, and teachers are busy with too many students to be able to give immediate reinforcement for good performance.

Skinner maintained that much learning, in both classrooms and the outside world, is controlled by positive reinforcement, but the efficiency and degree of learning could be improved greatly by attention to how and when reinforcers are administered. In other words, Skinner's "simple" concept, positive reinforcement, has widespread applications throughout society. If only the end results are seen (for example, operating complicated machinery and equipment, solving mathematical problems, playing sports skillfully, or using involved scientific methods), it is difficult to imagine how Skinner's analysis could be relevant. However, what must be remembered is that these behaviors are not acquired all at once. They are acquired step by step, sometimes efficiently, sometimes inefficiently.

According to Skinner, appropriately applied positive reinforcement (for example, immediate positive feedback for correct behavior) can foster enjoyable, rapid, and thorough learning. On the other hand, lack of appropriate, systematic reinforcement can make learning unpleasant, slow, and careless. (In many cases, "rules" also promote learning; for example, a person may receive verbal instructions regarding the operation of a machine or the application of a scientific procedure. Skinner referred to "rule-governed" behavior to indicate that it isn't always necessary for us to be exposed to actual circumstances in order to learn. Of course, rule-following behavior itself is affected by reinforcement: If following the instructions, advice, or warnings of others is reinforced, such behavior is strengthened. More will be said about this shortly.)

To refer back to an earlier paragraph, it's true that we all know that the salesperson's commissions, the student's grades, the attention a child gets, and so on can influence their behaviors. But simply to acknowledge these influences on behavior does not show that we understand all that Skinner meant when he discussed positive reinforcement. There are multitudes of positive reinforcers that operate in people's lives, some very obvious (like money, report cards, and orgasms) and others more subtle (like nods of approval, gentle touches, and casual complimentary remarks). Also, the consequences of behaviors such as turning doorknobs, reaching for objects, or moving one's head to increase visibility can be reinforcing. All of these can affect behavior. To Skinner, the details of how, when, and where reinforcers are received go a long way toward explaining human behavior in its simple and complex forms, at work, school, home, and elsewhere. The concept of positive reinforcement is more than an obvious version of common knowledge.

A few final comments can be made about simplicity and Skinner's psychology. First, as indicated in Chapter Two, there are a number of concepts beyond positive reinforcement that Skinner used to explain behavior: schedules of reinforcement, negative reinforcement, punishment, extinction, generalization, discrimination, contingencies of reinforcement, and so on.

Second, the complexity of operant-conditioning research (or, as it is often called, "the experimental analysis of behavior") has reached the stage where Skinner himself admitted that he didn't understand some of it. Current work on the relationships among situational factors, behaviors, and consequences is being done by many behaviorally oriented researchers, often using computers in their laboratories (for example, to provide intricate schedules of reinforcement). The published studies of such research often are so technical that they can be understood only by a small group of specialists.

Third, Skinner's concept of "rule-governed" behavior makes it clear that our actions can be affected by advice, suggestions, instructions, and other verbal stimuli, thereby including in his psychology influences that sometimes are mistakenly thought to be outside its realm. In his view, behavior often is determined by its consequences, but the consequences need not be experienced directly. Being told about consequences also can have an effect. Though much of our behavior is "contingency shaped" (shaped by direct consequences), the following of "rules" also is common. For example, as Skinner indicated, learning to drive a car involves both rule-governed and contingency-shaped behaviors. The learner is given verbal directions to supplement the natural consequences that result from behaviors such as depressing the clutch, moving the shift lever, pressing the accelerator, turning the steering wheel, and so on.

It's important to remember that rules themselves generally come about because of consequences that have occurred; they then describe, state, or imply behaviors and consequences to those who have not been exposed to the actual situations. If it were not for rule-governed behavior, each individual's behaviors would be influenced only by natural consequences. This would lead to many problems. As a simple example, imagine each driver's behaviors having to be shaped from the start strictly by real consequences.

Among rule-governed behaviors, Skinner included the effects of commands, advice, warnings, directions, instructions, folklore, proverbs, governmental and religious laws, and the laws of science. Our behaviors come under the influence of rules because of reinforcement for following them. In other words, just as we "learn" other behaviors, we also learn to follow rules. Also, we "trust" those who give us advice that, when followed, results in reinforcement; we will tend to follow their advice in the future.

A few more things need to be said about rule-governed behavior. Skinner saw it as "knowledge by description," whereas contingency-shaped behavior is "knowledge by acquaintance." Behavior influenced by rules often is relatively awkward when compared with behavior that has been brought under the control of actual consequences. In the example given above of a person learning to drive, the importance of verbal instructions is obvious; however, driving behavior will not be smooth and proficient until the person has had actual, firsthand driving experience (imagine taking a driving test for a license after having had only verbal instruction). Similarly, doing carpentry, riding a bicycle, conducting a scientific experiment, operating a computer, and growing fruits and vegetables (this list could go on and on) require more than rule-governed behavior (though suggestions, advice, instructions, and other "rules" can serve useful functions by influencing relevant behaviors); what is required for expertise is the development of contingency-shaped behaviors.

Skinner pointed out that learning in our schools primarily involves rule-governed behavior (it is knowledge by description). Such learning is most useful if the behavior is appropriate and is reinforced by actual consequences in the world outside the classroom; this results in acquiring knowledge by acquaintance. Major problems can occur when there is a long delay between classroom learning and "real-world" learning; for example, rule-governed behavior may not be sufficiently strong to survive the delay (it may extinguish before it is reinforced by direct, natural consequences).

Before we conclude this section, it may interesting to consider the following questions: Even if Skinner's approach were judged to be simple (which seems unjustified on the basis of what has been said here), is that necessarily bad? Is a complex approach inherently better than a simple one? Isn't it important to ask which approach is more useful? Skinnerian psychology has not yet proved itself to the point where all other approaches must immediately take a back seat, and it may indeed prove to be too simple to be *the* explanation for *all* human behavior. On the other hand, its successful applications indicate increasing possibilities.

So far we have discussed common misunderstandings related to the four major sources of controversy covered in Chapter Three. It is important to point out several additional ways in which Skinnerian psychology is sometimes misinterpreted. Specifically, we will consider the confusion of Skinner's approach with other approaches and will touch on what Skinner had to say about some issues that many times are mistakenly thought to have been ignored by him: feelings, thoughts, self-knowledge, self-control, and creativity.

Skinner's Approach versus Other Methods of Behavior Control

Skinner's emphasis when advocating behavior control was on the use of positive reinforcement. He suggested setting up environments in which persons behave in individually and socially beneficial ways because those behaviors are positively reinforced. Further, he recommended that we do this in a planned, systematic way and not leave "good" behavior to chance. (It isn't that we completely ignore the use of positive reinforcement now, but rather that we often use it in a haphazard way.) In looking at our society, Skinner saw that behavior often is controlled through aversive techniques and punishment. Instead of consistently and effectively using positive reinforcement to promote desirable and appropriate behaviors, those in positions of authority (teachers, parents, supervisors, employers) often resort to threats, reprimands, penalties, and so forth in order to control the behavior of those under them. Of course, you don't necessarily have to be in a position of authority to use aversive and punishing techniques; these techniques sometimes are used in return against authority figures and also in relationships among peers. Skinner clearly was against using such techniques of behavior control (though he acknowledged both the difficulty of avoiding all punitive practices and the fact that we do not always have appropriate nonpunitive methods to use). He advised that we try to maximize the use of positive reinforcement rather than using it in a now-and-then, hit-or-miss fashion.

The significant point here is that Skinner's program for controlling behavior rests on the use of positive reinforcement. This is not always clearly understood. People sometimes confuse Skinner's approach with other, unrelated approaches. Numerous magazine and newspaper articles have made this error. For example, a recent article in a very popular newsmagazine equated Skinner's methods with those of putting prisoners in solitary confinement, giving child molesters severe electric shocks in the groin while showing them pictures of naked children, and giving a drug that causes severe vomiting to mentally disturbed inmates who were caught lying or swearing. It even went on to include brain surgery for the criminally insane as a technique of behavior modification. The article drew a direct connection between these methods and the suggestions of Skinner. Nothing could be further from the truth. He had specifically and plainly disavowed any association with such techniques. Despite this, erroneous conclusions continue to be drawn about what Skinner had suggested, and often there is no acknowledgment that his proposals for behavior control focused on positive reinforcement.

Feelings and Thoughts

Another frequent misinterpretation of Skinner's psychology is that it ignores feelings and thoughts. "All that Skinner talked about is behavior and the environment. He didn't seem to believe that we have emotions or that we can think!" These types of comments are common. It's very true that he was a behaviorist, and a radical one at that. However, it isn't true that he denied the reality of feelings and thought processes. How could he? He himself had emotions and thoughts (despite what his more hostile critics have suggested). It would be rather absurd if he had said that these inner events do not exist. Not only do they exist, but "How people feel is often as important as what they do" (Skinner, 1989, p.3).

Though he acknowledged the importance of feelings and thoughts, Skinner did see them in a rather unique way: they have *no causal status* in his system of psychology. (This is a significant aspect of "radical behaviorism," a phrase often used by Skinner to refer to his views. A major reason why his position is "radical" is because feelings and thoughts are not considered to be causes of behavior, though he indicated that the nature of these processes does need to be analyzed.)

Most of us believe that much of our behavior is determined by our feelings and thoughts. For example, someone might say, "I worked hard today because I was in a good mood" or "I stayed home yesterday because I was depressed." Skinner would not accept these explanations of behavior. He would accept the fact that this person felt "good" today and "depressed" yesterday, but he would not go along with the notion that these feelings *caused* the person to either work hard or stay home. To Skinner, feelings do not cause behavior. Rather, the specifics of both feelings and behavior are determined by environmental circumstances. Both "feeling good" and "working hard" can be controlled by positive reinforcers, such as adequate pay, praise from supervisors, regular promotions, good relationships with coworkers, and the ability to do one's job effectively. Both "feeling depressed" and "staying home from work" can be controlled by aversive conditions, such as inadequate pay, criticism from supervisors, poor performance evaluations, disagreements with co-workers, and inability to do one's job effectively. Skinner advises that these types of environmental circumstances provide the key to explaining both our feelings *and* our behaviors.

Thinking also is controlled by the environment. For example, a person growing up in a wealthy family in New York City will have quite different thoughts from someone growing up in a very isolated area with parents who are barely scratching out a living. Although a very obvious example, it makes the point that particular thoughts are shaped by the social and physical environments to which the individual is exposed.

Humans, because of the genetic characteristics of the species, are capable of feeling and thinking. These capabilities are givens; just as we are capable of speaking, reading, picking up objects with our fingers, walking upright, and so on, we also are capable of feeling and thinking. However, according to Skinner, the *extent* to which we feel and think, and *what* we feel and think about, are determined by environmental conditions, especially the influence of other persons (who constitute what he called the "verbal community"). They question us about our feelings and thoughts ("How do you feel today?" or "What are you thinking?") and reinforce our responses with their attention and comments. Thereby, the activities of feeling and thinking become important to us. Some persons may become more "sensitive" or "introspective" than others because engaging in these activities has been more strongly reinforced.

As mentioned, what we feel and think also is influenced by the significant persons in our lives. To give a very simple example, the victory of a Democratic presidential candidate is likely to cause feelings of happiness and thoughts of prosperity among the members of a politically involved family who happen to be Democrats; they encourage and reinforce one another's political feelings and beliefs. On the other hand, the members of a staunch Republican family would be likely to experience despair and thoughts of economic deprivation after the Democratic victory because of their mutual encouragement and reinforcement of an alternative set of feelings and beliefs. Different environments result in differences in what is felt and thought.

The idea that feelings and thoughts control behavior is generally accepted in our society but was not accepted by Skinner. We easily accept explanations based on emotional and mental states: "She quit smoking because she wanted to"; "He's not going to the party because he feels sad"; "She finally decided to buy a car." These types of statements suggest that the reasons for behavior reside within the person. But we are left with having to explain why the first person "wants," why the second person is "sad," and why the third person "decided"; when such inner states are used to explain behavior, they are *explanatory fictions*—they explain nothing, according to Skinner. He would advise looking for the environmental conditions that are related to certain feelings or thoughts, as well as overt behaviors. A satisfactory explanation consists of finding the environmental events that control the ways we feel, think, *and* behave. (Actually, in Skinner's approach, feeling and thinking also can be considered behaviors. Though they occur "within the skin" and are not directly observable, they obey the same basic rules as our overt, public, observable behaviors; that is, they too are subject to environmental control.)

Self-Knowledge

In contemporary society we put a lot of emphasis on "knowing ourselves." It is commonly thought that to be able to understand our inner states is a strong virtue. Skinner suggested that there is a special problem in gaining this type of knowledge: those around us can't directly observe our internal conditions and therefore can't help us to label them consistently. For example, there's quite a difference between teaching children to differentiate among colors, shapes, symbols, and so on and teaching them to differentiate among the stimuli that arise within their bodies. In the latter case the stimuli are private, in the sense that others do not have direct access to them. These stimuli can be inferred only from what the individual says or does.

It is important to realize that Skinner did address the issue of self-knowledge, although he discussed it in materialistic terms. For him, the problem of "knowing ourselves" has to do with stimuli, responses, and reinforcement. It is not a matter of getting in touch with some deep inner self or developing some special internal quality.

Skinner approached the topic of self-knowledge by identifying the three nervous systems by which we respond to our bodies: (1) the *interoceptive system* carries stimuli from our digestive, respiratory, and circulatory systems; (2) the *proprioceptive system* carries stimuli from muscles, joints, tendons, and other organs involved in body postures and movements; and (3) the *exteroceptive system* carries the stimuli received from our bodies and our surroundings that are involved in seeing, hearing, tasting, touching, and smelling. These three systems are assumed to have developed during our evolutionary history because of their biological significance, but with the development of verbal communication they came to serve a new function: to answer questions about ourselves.

When we are asked by others about our feelings, sensations, perceptions, thoughts, and so on, we learn to observe our bodily states in response to these questions. Therefore, what often is referred to as "self-knowledge" is essentially the result of observations that we make of interoceptive and proprioceptive stimuli arising from within our bodies. These self-observations are brought about initially by persons who inquire about our inner states and reinforce certain of our responses with attention and approval. (As mentioned before, Skinner referred to these persons as the "verbal community".) If it weren't for these persons, there would be no self-knowledge. In short, Skinner suggested that observing and reporting on our inner states (more specifically, the stimuli that arise from our viscera, muscles, and so on) are behaviors that are shaped and maintained by the verbal community, and without this environmental influence there would be little reason to observe and report these internal events. Once self-observations have been reinforced, we then often make them on our own, even in the absence of immediate influences from other persons.

To return to an earlier point, Skinner believed that accurate self-knowledge is difficult to acquire. Since the verbal community doesn't have direct access to the relevant stimuli, it can't consistently provide reinforcement for making distinctions among the various ways we feel. If a teacher (a member of the verbal community) wants a child to differentiate between capital and lowercase letters, they both can look directly at the stimuli involved, and the teacher can consistently reinforce the correct responses. However, if the teacher wants the child to differentiate between "sadness" and "loneliness," the situation is more complicated. Only the child has access to the internal stimuli that can be labeled as either "feeling sad" or "feeling lonely." The teacher has to guess what the child is experiencing and therefore cannot consistently reinforce the child's distinctions. (If the external events that are affecting the child are known, the teacher can be more consistent.)

Because of this type of difficulty, Skinner suggested that we can't know what is going on inside of us as well as we can know external, objective events in the surrounding environment. Importantly, however, he believed that internal events and external events have a similar physical status. The former are simply "out of reach" for the verbal community, although they are immediate and intimate for the individual. Their immediacy and intimacy often result in the assignment of special qualities to inner stimuli, as though they define the "essence" or the "real personality" of the individual. Skinner obviously did not agree with such views of inner states. For him, they are to be explained in the same way overt events are explained: by referring to *stimuli, responses,* and the *consequences* that follow responses.

Self-Control

Skinner did not approach *self-control* in traditional fashion; it isn't the exercise of "willpower," nor does it involve "thinking through" a problem to come to a "rational decision" about the prudent course of action. Rather, it refers to behaviors that successfully change the probability of making some response. For example, some self-controlling behaviors reduce the chances of making a response that will be punished and are reinforced by the fact that they *do* reduce punishable responses.

In self-control, one response (the *controlling* response) alters the factors that control another response (the *controlled* response). The controlled response may be one that has conflicting consequences. In other words, it is capable of producing both positive and negative outcomes. For example, drinking alcoholic beverages, smoking cigarettes, and overeating are responses that can have both reinforcing consequences (such as physical pleasure and escape from boring circumstances) and punishing consequences (such as physical disorders and social censure). We often vacillate between doing these things and not doing them. If the consequences of doing them became sufficiently aversive, we are apt to "control ourselves." A typical observer might explain our controlling behavior by referring to our "decision" finally to exert some "willpower," but to Skinner the important determinant would be the aversive consequences that we escape or avoid.

Consider an example of a heavy smoker. He enjoys smoking, saying that it relaxes him, gives him a break from the routine at work, and in social situations gives him "something to do with his hands" (in other words, smoking has certain reinforcing outcomes for this person). On the other hand, he reads that smoking can cause heart and lung diseases, his doctor warns him about its ill effects and advises that he stop, his wife tells him that she worries about his health and also dislikes the smell of stale cigarette butts, and he begins to have coughing spells and finds that he gets out of breath easily. What will he do? Skinner's reasoning suggests that his actions will be determined by these various influences and that the idea of his "making a decision" to smoke or not smoke is illusory. If he quits and remains a nonsmoker, it is because of the reduction of punishing, aversive outcomes; refraining from smoking may be additionally reinforced by praise from his doctor, wife, and friends, by renewed physical abilities, and in other ways.

Skinner suggested that it is of little use to urge people to use "willpower" or to "take personal responsibility" for their behavior. He believed that these methods of encouraging self-control are not likely to have strong effects (though they may provide more aversive stimulation that the person can reduce by controlling his or her behaviors and in that way may contribute to self-control). According to Skinner, it is more effective to teach techniques for controlling undesirable behaviors. These techniques can be taught in the same way as any other skill—that is, by reinforcing appropriate responses. Individuals can learn to avoid tempting situations, to "do something else" that is incompatible with undesirable behavior (for example, an overweight person might exercise instead of eating), to use physical restraint (for example, a nail biter might keep his hands in his pockets), and so on. Appropriate techniques of self-control need to be taught to each individual for his or her own particular problems.

Creativity

Despite the common belief that Skinner had nothing to say about *creativity,* he did discuss it. Again, however, his reasoning was not traditional. He didn't account for creativity by referring to "creative impulses" or "ingenious uses of inner resources." As with other behaviors, Skinner suggested that creativity is the result of a person's genetic endowment and environmental experiences.

When someone does something "creative" (for example, invents a new tool, discovers a new solution for an old problem, paints a beautiful picture, or writes an inspiring poem), we often think that he or she has some special inner quality. Skinner's analysis points instead toward special experiences that have interacted with the person's genetic endowment to produce unique behaviors. Therefore, instead of giving the person credit, his or her environment and genes deserve the credit.

Though creative acts sometimes seem somewhat mysterious, as though they occur spontaneously and almost impulsively, it must be remembered that the persons involved generally have complex histories of reinforcement for a wide variety of behaviors. Many situations in which creativity takes place are not totally new or unfamiliar. Even in situations in which there seems to be little similarity with the person's previous experiences, there may be subtle common elements to which the person responds. If the individual has a large behavioral repertoire relevant to the project at hand, he or she will "try out" various behaviors until a "creative act" finally emerges.

An observer might notice only the final behavioral product and admire the sudden act of creativity. This is understandable, because the process leading to it sometimes occurs very quickly. Much of the process may occur covertly, since on the basis of previous experiences the creative person can think about various possible behaviors and their outcomes. "Thinking" in this sense is simply behaving, but at a level at which it can't be observed by others. (Remember, Skinner did not deny thought processes; he believed, however, that the specifics of what we think are determined by our experiences, that our thoughts are not "free," and that thinking is not a cause of behavior. Thinking may serve as a substitute for carrying out behaviors at the overt level; it is similar but occurs "inside the skin.")

Some creative behaviors do occur quite spontaneously and don't necessarily follow the process just mentioned. To explain these behaviors, Skinner referred to "mutations" and selection. He likened his ideas to those of Darwin's theory of evolution. During the evolutionary process, certain genetic mutations are selected because of their survival value. In a similar sense, certain behavioral mutations occur and are selected because they are successful (reinforcing). For example, an artist who uses a different brush stroke or an inventor who changes the design of a machine is producing mutations that may survive (be selected) if they are "pleasing" or "useful" (that is, if they are reinforcing).

Mutations can result from "accidents" (such as when an artist picks up the wrong brush and begins using it or when an inventor makes a beneficial mistake in design), or they can be variations due to the reinforcement involved in "doing things differently." In the latter case, there are artists, inventors, musicians, writers, and other creative individuals who have received attention and praise for varying their approaches, and therefore they continue to be "creative" by exploring new ground. Also, their "creative" behaviors may be reinforced simply by the new effects that they produce (that is, the reinforcers are not necessarily social ones).

Skinner suggested that creative persons have been exposed to environmental circumstances that have molded their creativity. According to him, we do what we do, creative or not, because of the consequences of our behaviors or because of consequences that have been described to us. Creative behaviors are impressive because of their novelty, and often they make the average person feel that "I never could have done that because I'm just not that original or unique." What may be missing for the average person, however, is not some special inner quality but, rather, some "original" or "unique" past and present environmental circumstances. If the creative person's experiences could be duplicated exactly in all their subtle as well as obvious details, it is likely that creativity would also be duplicated (assuming that genetic endowments didn't differ significantly). But would it still be "creativity"?

This chapter has been concerned with misunderstandings about Skinner's psychology. To summarize some of the major points: (1) Skinner opposed the traditional concept of self-determination, but he supported the ideals of individual achievement and satisfaction within a strong society; (2) he was a determinist but acknowledged the possibilities of unpredictability and the meaningfulness of individual actions; (3) he strongly advocated the systematic control of behavior through control of environmental conditions, but he also emphasized the need for countercontrol; (4) he initially developed his concepts from rat and pigeon studies, but many applications at the human level have been successful; (5) his concept of positive reinforcement may appear simplistic, but its applications are broad and often lead to the conditioning of complex behaviors; (6) his approach to behavior control emphasizes the use of positive reinforcement and does *not* advocate aversive control, punishment, or brain surgery as means of controlling behaviors; (7) he suggested that particular feelings and thoughts are *not* causes of behavior but, rather, are themselves determined (in a manner similar to overt behaviors) by environmental conditions; (8) he explained self-knowledge, self-control, and creativity in behavioral terms, emphasizing that these activities are controlled by environmental conditions (mainly by behavioral *consequences*), rather than resulting from inner qualities or states of mind.

FIVE

Views on Sigmund Freud

B. F. SKINNER was born in 1904 and died in 1990, grew up in the small American town of Susquehanna, Pennsylvania, graduated from Harvard University's doctoral program in psychology, devoted much of his life to laboratory research, and was an advocate of radical behaviorism. Sigmund Freud was born in 1856 and died in 1939, grew up in the European city of Vienna, graduated from the University of Vienna's medical school, spent much of his life analyzing mental disorders, and was the founder of psychoanalysis. What do these two men of such different backgrounds have in common?

Both have had a tremendous impact on the field of psychology, have gained widespread public attention, and have stirred up a large amount of controversy by challenging the traditional views of their times. In addition, they share these characteristics: (1) *an intense interest in understanding behavior;* whether it be Skinner's rats pressing levers or Freud's patients telling their dreams, attention is devoted to the causes of behavior; (2) *an emphasis on the study of individual organisms rather than groups;* though both wrote about group behavior, Skinner's laboratory research focused on the behaviors of individual rats or pigeons isolated in Skinner boxes, and Freud concentrated on individual patients undergoing analysis in the privacy of his office; (3) *a concern with the extension of their findings to social problems;* despite the fact that the research of both focused on individual organisms, their writings reflect great interest in applying their findings more broadly—in fact, to society as a whole; (4) *the belief that humans essentially are not rational decision makers;* Skinner believed that it is our genes and the environment, rather than rational decisions, that cause us to behave as we do, and Freud believed that we are strongly influenced by unconscious, irrational motives; (5) *the belief that behavior is determined in a lawful way by natural causes;* rather than believing that behaviors occur haphazardly or mysteriously, they both stressed that there is an underlying orderliness determined by the nature of humans and the world in which we live.

Though Skinner and Freud share some common characteristics, there also are some striking differences. These differences will become clear in the following sections as we take a look at what Skinner said about Freud. He set himself apart from Freud in a number of important ways. Here and there I have used examples that I believe accurately represent Skinner's meanings.

The "Mental Apparatus"

Skinner (1972) wrote that an important contribution of Freud's was to reduce "the sphere of accident and caprice in our considerations of human conduct" (p. 239). In other words, Freud was a determinist, and Skinner agreed with the value of this approach. Freud analyzed many behaviors that previously were thought either too insignificant to consider or too complex to explain. He found reasons for minor behaviors such as slips of the tongue, errors in writing, and the forgetting of names or appointments, as well as more dramatic behaviors such as fainting, nightmares, loss of the use of a limb despite the absence of a physical problem, and uncontrollable fears of harmless animals or objects. He took the approach that naturalistic explanations are possible. He didn't give up easily and simply say something like: "Well, I guess there's no way of explaining that; it's just something mysterious that happens."

Although praising Freud's determination to find the causes of various behaviors, Skinner suggested that he spent too much time looking in the wrong place. Freud's wasted efforts, in Skinner's view, were due to his construction of a "mental apparatus" to account for behavior. This apparatus consists primarily of the well-known triad—id, ego, and superego. The *id* refers to primitive human tendencies: basic instincts and repressed, irrational wishes and impulses, all of which are unconscious. The *ego* is the realistic aspect of the personality. It attempts to satisfy the id's demands while also meeting the requirements of reality and the moral prescriptions of the *superego,* which includes the conscience. Freud often referred to these internal systems when explaining behavior. The id's instincts could result in impulsive behavior, the ego's realistic processes could result in rational behavior, and the superego could cause moralistic behavior.

It isn't completely clear how Freud meant these internal personality mechanisms to be used. He varied his own usage of them. In some of his writings it seems that the id is meant to stand for human genetic inheritance, whereas the ego and superego refer to what persons learn as they are socialized. In other writings, Freud slips away from this usage, and the id, ego, and superego assume a reality of their own, as though they actually exist within the person and determine behavior. (Perhaps they are best considered as concepts representing the major aspects of the human personality as viewed by Freud.)

According to Skinner, there is an inherent danger in using mentalistic concepts for explaining behavior. They tend to become *the* explanations, in and of themselves. In actuality, they can never be real explanations because they themselves have to be explained. (Skinner calls such concepts "explanatory fictions"—they seem to explain behavior but in fact explain nothing.) If individuals are said to do things because of irrational wishes of the id, rational ideas of the ego, or moralistic values of the superego, the question remains as to how the wishes, ideas, and values originated. That question carries the explanation back to environmental influences (some experience or set of experiences that the person has had) or to some genetic factor. To Skinner, one's environmental experiences and genetic endowment are the determinants that have to be taken into account, and mentalistic concepts get in the way of the pursuit of these critical factors. (Though including genetic factors as behavioral determinants, Skinner himself concentrated on the study of current environmental factors because they are more directly observable and more easily altered.)

Skinner suggested that Freud's failure to stick with environmental determinism, and his commitment to a determinism that mixes mentalistic concepts with environmental factors, resulted in considerable damage. Though Freud seemed at times to recognize the dangers of using concepts such as id, ego, and superego, he chose to use them anyway. As a result, his and his followers' pursuit of environmental determinants of behavior has been seriously hindered. Skinner explained this by noting that the Freudian explanatory system involves three steps: (1) an *external environmental event* (some experience) produces (2) an *internal mental state* (such as an emotion, idea, or conflict) that results in (3) some *observable behavior*. For example, certain traumatic environmental events of early childhood can produce long-lasting inner conflicts that can cause adult neurotic behaviors.

What's wrong with this three-link causal chain? Skinner illustrated the problem with an example of *punishment* for childhood sexual behavior, which produces *anxiety* or *guilt*, which then supposedly causes *unusual adult sexual behaviors*. He believed that the middle link isn't needed and, furthermore, it confuses matters. For him, the actual explanation for the adult's unusual sexual behaviors is the punishment incident, not the anxiety or guilt (they too would be caused by the punishment—they are not causes themselves, but effects). Through the introduction of the middle link of anxiety or guilt, attention tends to get drawn away from the significant environmental event (punishment).

Also, Skinner pointed out that inner states such as anxiety or guilt have a tendency to steal the *whole* show. Not only do they detract from the investigation of environmental events, but they cloud the detailed study of the behavioral outcomes of these events. In other words, anxiety or guilt becomes so central that the important question of exactly what the person is *doing* (or not doing) gets slighted. Specifically, in our example, it is important to know precisely what the unusual sexual behaviors are, how often they occur, and under what circumstances they occur. This type of information clarifies the problem. If anxiety, guilt, or some other inner state becomes the center of attention, it is easy to forget to observe the details of the problem behavior.

Skinner was disturbed by our tendency to look *within* for answers to our behavioral problems, and he believed that Freud contributed greatly to this tendency. How many times have you heard someone discuss anxieties, fears, inner conflicts, and so on? We frequently use these kinds of concepts to explain our own behaviors as well as those of other persons. But are we really explaining anything, or are we using "explanatory fictions"? Wouldn't it clarify things and be more helpful to focus on the specific observable behaviors that indicate what we call anxiety, fear, or conflict, rather than referring to some vague, unobservable inner state? Second, wouldn't it be beneficial to consider how the environment can be changed to bring about more desirable behaviors? Skinner advocated this two-step process, rather than the three-step process of Freud. For Skinner, it is essential to identify the relationships between environmental conditions and behaviors (the contingencies of reinforcement). He saw Freud as having confused things by insisting on an intermediate mental apparatus.

Does this mean that Skinner ignored our mental processes and denied that we feel, think, have doubts, suffer from anxieties and guilt, and so on? The answer, as was made clear earlier, is "No." He acknowledged that we experience these states, but he didn't see them as being in the causal chain. *They are effects, not causes.* The specifics of what we feel and think are controlled by environmental conditions, just as overt observable behaviors are.

Skinner pointed out two major problems that arise if mentalistic concepts are considered as explanations of behavior. First, *how can mental states be observed?* They cannot be studied objectively. This is a serious issue in developing a science of behavior. Of course, mental processes can be inferred from what people say they are thinking or feeling, but such statements often are inconsistent and have doubtful accuracy. Skinner suggested that behavioral scientists should look directly for the environmental conditions that affect behavior, rather than looking for causes in the inner experiencing of those conditions. According to his view, persons react to the environment, not to their inner states. Inner processes do exist, but they too are environmentally influenced.

Second, *how can mental states be altered directly?* This is an important question for psychoanalysts and other therapists, since they often focus on changing their patients' feelings, thoughts, expectations, and other inner states. (For example, Freud emphasized the necessity of developing the inner quality of "a strong ego.") In Skinner's view, there is no such thing as *directly* changing an inner state. If patients develop better feelings and clearer thoughts, it is because their environmental conditions and behaviors have changed, regardless of what the therapist or patient believes is the cause of the improvement. Therapy sessions themselves may provide a changed environment, and therapists additionally may suggest things that patients can do in their everyday lives to alter their situations (thereby encouraging rule-governed behavior). Skinner's reasoning suggests that these changes actually are the factors that bring therapeutic results, even though they may seem incidental or secondary in importance to the therapist's goal of working on the patient's feelings or thinking processes.

Following Skinner's advice, it would be most efficient to go directly to environmental conditions and behaviors, instead of complicating the therapeutic process by attempting to deal with the patient's inner states. "Take care of the person's environment and behavior, and his (her) inner condition will take care of itself " is one way of putting Skinner's theme. When using techniques based on Skinner's ideas, behavior therapists help their clients improve their circumstances, behaviors, and behavioral consequences (that is, they try to change the "contingencies of reinforcement"). When these improve, better feelings and thoughts also are likely to occur. As a simple example, receiving positive reinforcement (such as approval from the therapist or others) not only can shape and strengthen improved behaviors but also can produce "good feelings." As the client progresses, more and more effective behaviors develop; these behaviors, and the consequences they produce, help to sustain the client's "healthy mental and emotional state."

Skinner's criticisms of Freud's use of mentalistic concepts are not meant to negate Freud's accomplishments completely. Freud made many interesting observations that connected childhood experiences to adult behaviors, and Skinner appreciated the importance of these observations. Also, he acknowledged that patients sometimes improve during psychoanalysis and related therapies. However, he suggested that, rather than being explained by psychoanalytic notions, these successes are related to the altering of the patient's environment and behavior. For example, for the first time the patient may be in a situation in which he or she can say anything without being criticized or judged; suppressed fears may be expressed and eventually extinguished because they produce no negative or other consequences in the protective therapeutic environment. The fact that the analyst provides a "nonpunishing audience" may be a critical environmental factor that determines the patient's "cure."

Skinner's main point was that Freud would have been *more* effective in both theorizing and doing therapy, and his ideas would have led to *less* confusion and wasted effort, if he had never used mentalistic concepts. In Skinner's opinion, Freud should have stuck to the study of the details of behavior (how, when, and where it occurs) and to the consequences of those behaviors. (In essence, Skinner was saying that Freud should have been a behaviorist.)

The Unconscious

Another aspect of Freudian psychology that Skinner criticized is the concept of the *unconscious mind.* Freud divided the mind into three levels of consciousness: (1) the *conscious,* which includes all that we are aware of at a particular time, (2) the *preconscious,* which consists of material that can be brought to the conscious level relatively easily if we concentrate on it, and (3) the *unconscious* which contains material of which we are unaware but that nevertheless affects our behavior. It is the unconscious, according to Freud, that primarily dominates our personalities. It contains instinctive sexual and aggressive impulses, forbidden wishes and desires, unpleasant memories, and other elements that churn away below the surface and push us in various directions. (There is overlap between the concepts of the unconscious and the id. The id is considered to be totally unconscious and therefore the reservoir of much of the material at that level.) Freud's psychoanalytic techniques are designed to tap the unconscious so that disturbing material can be revealed and "worked through" (which involves coming to terms with long-hidden impulses, wishes, conflicts, and so on). The two main techniques that Freud used to accomplish this were *dream interpretation* (psychoanalysts consider dreams to be indicators of unconscious wishes) and *free association* (the patient is told to relax and to say whatever comes to mind; this is intended to allow unconscious material to surface gradually).

Skinner considered the unconscious to be a misleading concept. He objected primarily to Freud's idea that the unconscious has a *causal* role in determining behavior, a central theme in Freud's theory of human behavior and in his psychoanalytic therapy. Skinner maintained that behavior is determined by genetic and environmental factors and that there is no reason to assign special importance to the person's state of awareness regarding these factors. We are aware (conscious) of some of these factors and unaware (unconscious) of others, but the implication of Skinner's line of reasoning is "So what?" To him, our awareness or lack of awareness of the genetic and environmental factors that influence us is incidental, *having no causal significance.*

Simply stated, Skinner suggested that it doesn't matter whether or not we are aware of the factors that act on us; they still exist and have an effect. Therefore, Freud's elevation of the unconscious to a position of unique significance is unwarranted. It causes misplaced efforts to "analyze" the unconscious, when what really needs analyzing are the genetic and (especially) the environmental factors that cause individuals to behave as they do. The degree of awareness that people have about these factors is not what causes their behaviors. In fact, according to Skinner, awareness itself is a type of behavior; thus it is an effect rather than a cause.

To give an example, among some people there is great emphasis on "knowing yourself" Questions such as "How do you feel about that?" or "What are you thinking?" are asked often, and certain responses are reinforced with attention and approval. Similarly, from a Skinnerian perspective, a psychoanalyst attempts to get patients to become more aware of past and present conditions that affect their behavior and reinforces them with attention and approval (perhaps by mentioning that progress is being made) when they make appropriate descriptive statements about these conditions. In this way, what was previously "unconscious" becomes "conscious." Skinner acknowledged that people are capable of some degree of self-awareness (self-observation) because of human genetic inheritance, but he believed that this type of behavior actually occurs only when it is encouraged and reinforced by our fellow human beings (the "verbal community"). Some persons become more "aware" than others because they have more experiences in which awareness is reinforced. To quote Skinner (1987b) directly: "All behavior . . . is unconscious; it becomes 'conscious' when verbal environments provide the contingencies necessary for self-observation" (p. 782).

It's interesting to consider that both Skinner and Freud would agree that we don't have to be aware of our behavior or its determinants in order to carry out actions. All of us do certain things without consciously knowing why we do them, sometimes without even realizing what we are doing. When our attention is called to such actions, we might say that we do them "automatically," "without thinking" or "impulsively," or we might even deny that we do them at all. Though both Skinner and Freud agree that such behaviors exist, they disagree about their importance.

To review and summarize Skinner's position, he suggested simply that sometimes we are aware of our behavior and its causes, and sometimes we are not, depending on what our experiences have been. Some persons are encouraged frequently by others (such as parents, peers, or psychoanalysts) to observe their own behaviors, and doing so is often reinforced. Therefore the behavior of being aware of what they are doing and why they are doing it becomes conditioned, and they make more self-observations than those who have had fewer such experiences. In either case, Skinner would argue that awareness is not a determinant of behavior. It is itself a behavior and is subject to the same rules as other behaviors: if making self-observations (being aware) is reinforced, it will continue to occur.

Freud, on the other hand, chose to place the unconscious at the center of both his theorizing and his analytic procedures with patients. In his view, unconscious factors affect the behaviors of both normal and neurotic individuals to varying extents, though his main focus was on neurotic behaviors. He believed that, to overcome negative unconscious influences, we must develop an awareness of these disturbing elements, and this could occur adequately only through the process of psychoanalysis. By bringing disturbing *unconscious* material to the *conscious* level and then "working it through" to remove its irrational, emotional grip on us, we can change our neurotic behaviors.

Freud clearly felt that it can make a difference in our behavior if we become aware of previously unconscious factors, and this is a point on which he and Skinner disagreed. Skinner suggested that such awareness is not critical and that our behaviors are affected by environmental and genetic factors, whether or not awareness of these factors exists. Currently this is a controversial issue, even among behaviorists. There is evidence indicating that certain self-monitoring or self-observation procedures can influence behavior. For example, sometimes simply counting and keeping a record of the frequency of a certain behavior—smoking eating, swearing, and so on—can affect its frequency. These procedures often are taught by behavior therapists and behavior modifiers. However, they are considered to be useful behaviors that clients are capable of learning, not methods for "probing the unconscious" or "discovering underlying conflicts."

The fact that self-monitoring or self-observation can influence behavior seems to challenge Skinner's suggestion that awareness is *not* a critical factor affecting behavior. However, consider the hypothetical example (mine, not Skinner's) of a man who is a heavy smoker. He is told by a behavior therapist to keep a daily record of the number of cigarettes smoked, and he then does so (rule-governed behavior). At the end of the day he lights up a cigarette and proceeds to total up the number of checkmarks he has made. Seeing that he smoked 45 cigarettes, he puts out the one he is holding. What has happened? One interpretation is that he is now "aware" of how much he is smoking and that "awareness" causes him to put out the cigarette. A Skinnerian interpretation, however, might be that he put out the cigarette because an aversive event (seeing that he smoked 45 cigarettes) followed "lighting up," and this suppressed his smoking behavior. This interpretation does not focus on "awareness" as the causal factor affecting smoking behavior; rather, it focuses on the effects of an aversive event.

To assume that awareness is necessary in this example is to add a factor that may be an explanatory fiction; it may be possible to leave it out of the following statement: "Seeing the number 45 led to awareness, which led to a reduction in smoking." The Skinnerian statement would be simply: "Seeing the number 45 suppressed smoking." Obviously, the example given is oversimplified; it is meant only to illustrate the *possibility* of a Skinnerian interpretation of behavior that appears, on the surface, to be explainable only by referring to an inner process of "awareness."

Getting back to Skinner's views on Freud, he suggested that Freud's own observation that we can be affected by unconscious factors (such as forgotten traumatic childhood incidents and biological events within our bodies) could have led Freud to the more general conclusion that degree of awareness is *not* a causal factor in determining behavior. In other words, if we can be influenced by factors of which we are unaware, then awareness itself should not be a critical factor. However, that is not what Freud concluded, and it is not what guided his efforts. He made strong distinctions between conscious and unconscious processes and indicated that significant behavioral outcomes were related to these different states. But this opened up another question: by what specific mechanism do states of awareness affect behavior? In Skinner's opinion, Freud did not supply an adequate answer.

Skinner's advice is to look for environmental determinants of our behaviors, but such determinants are less exciting and dramatic than Freud's. Our cultural experiences have made guilt, anxiety, uncontrollable impulses, hidden desires, forbidden wishes, and other presumably unconscious motives for behavior much more stimulating to consider and discuss. The greatest disadvantage of our interest in these types of explanations, in Skinner's opinion, is that they are explanatory fictions—we explain nothing by referring to these inner states. However fascinating they may be, they too have to be explained, and that requires the hard work of considering how our genes and experiences have brought these states into being.

Defense Mechanisms

In Freudian psychology, defense mechanisms are devices that are used unconsciously by the ego to cope with anxiety. Essentially, their use (especially if they are used extensively for a prolonged period) indicates a weak ego that is incapable of dealing realistically with the impulses and wishes of the id, the moralistic demands of the superego, and the external pressures from the environment. These forces can generate increasing amounts of anxiety if they aren't handled in some rational way. The inadequate ego therefore has to resort to the use of unrealistic, irrational defenses to try to deal with this anxiety. Defense mechanisms involve distortions or denials of the actual internal or external conditions that exist for the person. Skinner believed that the behaviors that Freud would have called "defensive" can be explained without referring to some action of an inner ego. Once again, Skinner relied on external conditions to explain behavior, whereas Freud referred to inner processes. Let's consider briefly three of the Freudian defense mechanisms and the explanation that Skinner gave of each.

Repression was said by Freud to be the "cornerstone" or "foundation stone" of psychoanalysis. As a defense mechanism, it refers to the exclusion of unacceptable or unpleasant thoughts, experiences, impulses, or other material from consciousness, and it explains why persons refrain from certain actions. For example, it might be said of someone that "He is repressing his desire to have an extramarital affair." Skinner suggested that the so-called effects of repression can be explained by referring to punishment. If persons have been punished or are under the threat of punishment for some behavior, they can avoid aversive consequences by not engaging in the forbidden behavior (such as an extramarital relationship) and by avoiding even the thought of it. For Skinner, it is unnecessary and misleading to use the concept of repression; external conditions (punishment or the threat of punishment) can explain why someone avoids doing or thinking about certain things.

Reaction formation is a defense mechanism that involves doing the opposite (often to an extreme) of what is unconsciously felt or thought. For example, unconscious resentment of a friend may be replaced with exaggerated displays of affection, or hidden sexual impulses may be covered up by extreme concern about morality. The ego attempts to protect against the anxiety that would result if the real feelings came to the surface. In Skinner's view, however, people respond to environmental circumstances, and it isn't necessary to bring in the concept of the ego using a "reaction formation." Basically, the individual will behave in ways that reduce the chances of being punished. If the threat of punishment is severe or persistent, action may be taken to "make certain" that the punishable behavior does not occur. In the first example above, dramatic displays of affection toward a friend make resentful behavior unlikely, and punishing outcomes (loss of the friendship, bitter reprisals, and so on) are avoided. Also, it is likely that affectionate behaviors will be reinforced by the friend's positive reactions. In the second example, constant expressions of moral concern make sexual opportunities unlikely to be presented, and therefore a recurrence of punishment (which perhaps occurred during childhood) is avoided. Also, expressions of moral concern may be reinforced by attention and affirmation from others. In these explanations, individuals are seen as being controlled by environmental circumstances, primarily the consequences of particular behaviors, rather than as being influenced by the inner workings of their egos.

Sublimation is a defense mechanism that, compared to repression, reaction formation, and others, has more positive benefits for the person and society. Freud suggested that the advance of culture is based on sublimation. The ego directs the energy of unconscious impulses into productive and creative activities. Basic sexual and aggressive drives are diverted into work and artistic pursuits, as well as other socially desirable behaviors. By accomplishing this, the ego reduces the buildup of tensions at the unconscious level and thereby lessens anxiety.

Simply put, sublimation involves "draining off" unconscious energy by using it for constructive purposes.

Obviously, Skinner didn't go along with this explanation based on inner, ego-directed processes. He suggested that being deprived of opportunities to emit certain reinforced behaviors may result in related behaviors being emitted and strengthened. For example, if deprived of opportunities for sexual behavior, a person may paint pictures of nude human bodies. In another case, a childless couple may treat a pet as if it were a child; in the presence of a stimulus (the pet) that bears certain similarities to a child (they both require care), the couple emits parental behavior. Where Freud was likely to see "sublimations of unconscious wishes," Skinner was likely to see conditions of deprivation and the generalization of responses (as in the case of painting pictures instead of engaging in sexual activities) or stimuli (as in the case when the stimulus "pet" has effects similar to the stimulus "child").

Skinner also indicated that if two types of behavior (perhaps sexual activity and athletic performance) have been reinforced and one of them is then punished, the other is more likely to occur. This is another possible explanation of some instances that Freud might have considered as sublimations of energy into alternative activities.

Persons who devote enormous amounts of time to their work might be considered as "sublimating" in Freud's terms, but they could also be viewed as individuals whose work behaviors are strengthened and maintained by money, by what is produced, by the attention and approval of others, or by other reinforcers. Skinner also offered another explanation: many people work hard in order to escape negative consequences, such as criticism or lack of money to buy essential goods. Again, we have the distinction between Freud's *inner* determinants and Skinner's *environmental* determinants.

Psychotherapy

Skinner acknowledged Freud's strong impact on current therapeutic methods. As indicated earlier, he believed that therapists influenced by Freud typically represent a "nonpunishing audience." They avoid criticizing or judging their patients. As therapy progresses, patients behave more and more in ways that they have avoided previously. They may recall unpleasant memories, be critical of other persons (including the therapist), act in hostile or selfish ways, cry, have violent outbursts, and so on. If the therapist continues to be nonpunishing, feelings such as guilt, fear, and anxiety may gradually diminish, and undesirable behaviors may decrease.

This behavioral explanation of the effectiveness of "traditional" psycho-therapies (that is, Freudian and related therapies) is based on the following assumptions: Many persons who seek therapy have emotional and behavioral problems caused by the widespread use of punishment and aversive control in our society. Authority figures (such as parents, teachers, and employers), social institutions (such as religious organizations and government agencies), and one's associates as well often rely on the use of punishment or threatened punishment to control behavior. Especially likely to produce problems for the individual are excessive or inconsistent uses of these controlling techniques. The traditional therapist provides a unique experience for such persons by being *consistently nonpunishing.* Troublesome emotions and undesirable behaviors that the patient has used to escape and avoid aversive conditions are thereby allowed to extinguish. To put it very simply, these undesirable emotional and behavioral responses subside when conditions make them unnecessary, and the nonpunishing therapist helps to establish those conditions.

Clearly, Skinner believed that the problems most patients bring to therapy result from the detrimental environmental conditions to which they have been exposed. What therapists need to do, in his view, is help construct new conditions for their patients that will bring about and maintain beneficial *behavioral* changes, which will have the accompanying effect of improving patients' emotional responses. He suggested that, even though traditional therapies are sometimes helpful, they aren't based on this view of the therapist's task. According to Skinner (1953): "The field of psychotherapy is rich in explanatory fictions" (pp. 372–373). Problem *behavior* is not examined as important subject matter in and of itself but rather is thought of as an indication of some underlying disorder, such as anxiety. Thus the patient's anxiety (an explanatory fiction) is treated, rather than the patient's behavior.

Freud fostered the belief that unusual behavior is merely the symptom of an inner neurotic condition that must be removed if behavior is to be changed. This reasoning is similar to that of the physician who treats an infection in order to cure its symptoms, and often it is referred to as the "disease model" or the "medical model" of mental illness. Skinner (1953) said that "this doctrine has given psychotherapy an impossible assignment" (p. 373); the assumed "inner cause" can't be observed objectively and can't be altered directly. It is the "symptoms" (the actual behaviors) that need to be worked on, not the internal states. By suggesting this, Skinner did not ignore the emotions of the person; by working on observable behaviors, the circumstances under which behaviors occur, and the consequences of behaviors (that is, by focusing on contingencies of reinforcement), emotions also will be affected. In other words, environmental and behavioral changes are accompanied by emotional changes. This view differs from that of Freud, who saw emotions as causes of behavior. To Skinner, both overt behavior and inner emotional responses are products of environmental influences.

The therapeutic techniques advocated by Freud are aimed at rooting out the inner source of the patient's problems. Skinner pointed out the similarity between this and the notion that unusual behavior is due to "possession" by the Devil—and that the Devil must be exorcised from the body before the person can be cured. Instead of the Devil, there are "anxieties, conflicts, repressed wishes, and repressed memories" (Skinner, 1953, p. 374) in Freudian psychology, and these must be discovered and resolved so that the patient's behavioral symptoms will be relieved. While doing this, the therapist also brings about changes in the patient's environment. Skinner believed that the patient is benefited by these *incidental* changes, rather than by the rooting out of inner problems.

Instead of incidental changes, Skinner suggested the systematic use of behavioral procedures to locate and change the environmental conditions related to troublesome, maladaptive behaviors. To do this, therapists need to get away from the traditional idea of underlying disorders and adopt the view that problem behaviors are strongly influenced by their consequences and accompanying environmental circumstances. This view leads to the next step: helping persons change their circumstances, behaviors, and the reinforcing consequences of their behaviors (again, we are talking about contingencies of reinforcement).

Behaviors that are maladaptive or troublesome may need to be *extinguished*. During therapy sessions or in the person's everyday life, situations can be set up so that these behaviors are no longer reinforced. At the same time, more desirable behaviors can be shaped through *positive reinforcement*. These goals often are accomplished by clients themselves upon advice from a behavior therapist. Here again, the concept of rule-governed behavior is important: the client's behavior may be changed by the therapist's advice or suggestions; if these changes are reinforced, the progress of therapy will be facilitated. In common terms, the client will "trust" the therapist and continue to go along with his or her advice.

Looking briefly at a hypothetical case, suppose a person comes for therapy because he is having troubles with his wife, his job, and his social relationships. He complains a great deal and says that he feels very anxious at times, with depression and guilt at other times. A traditional therapist would be likely to focus a good deal of attention on the anxiety, depression, and guilt, believing these disturbed inner states to be, in strong measure, the causes of the person's problem behaviors. Behavior therapists who have been influenced by Skinner's suggestions commonly have a different perspective, viewing anxiety, depression, and guilt as the results of aversive environmental conditions and maladaptive behaviors. These therapists tend to pinpoint specific behaviors that need to be changed and tend not to focus strongly on inner states. In the case being discussed, a behavior therapist might gather details on the ways in which the man interacts with others and then have him rehearse better ways of interacting, while *reinforcing* his progress with attention and approval. Meanwhile, the therapist might help to *extinguish* the man's unconstructive complaining by not encouraging it when it occurs and by changing to constructive discussions and the practicing of effective behavior. Additionally, the therapist would be likely to help him plan various changes in his everyday life in order to bring about more constructive, adaptive behaviors and to ensure the reinforcement of such behaviors.

A question might be: "What happens to the anxiety, depression, and guilt?" Skinner's reasoning is that discomforting feelings will change when the person's circumstances, behaviors, and behavioral consequences change. Anxiety, depression, and guilt commonly result from an individual's history of poor behavioral consequences. For example, if someone has been unsuccessful in his or her interpersonal relationships, usually a number of punishing outcomes for behaviors have occurred, producing behavioral and emotional problems (also, when relationships end, "despair" or "discouragement" often results because of lost reinforcers). When the person becomes more successful—that is, when behaviors bring positive reinforcement instead of punishment—better feelings will result.

Finally, does the therapeutic approach advocated by Skinner deal *only* with symptoms, rather than with basic, underlying causes? This is a question that has been raised by Freudian therapists who feel that behavior therapy is superficial. They believe that there is an internal cause for emotional and behavioral problems and that this cause must be discovered and dealt with before the person can expect permanent relief. Though admitting that behavior therapists may temporarily improve their patients, they argue that "symptom substitution" is likely. That is, a problem behavior may be changed, but some other problem will emerge because the underlying conflict, repressed trauma, or other basic inner cause has not been treated. (This argument is based on the "disease model," mentioned earlier.) Skinner didn't give any weight to this line of reasoning. He believed that, like it or not, a therapist always ends up dealing with basic *environmental conditions* and *behavioral changes,* even when he or she thinks that "underlying problems" are being treated. (As a last note to this discussion of symptom substitution: Behavior therapists have conducted a number of studies to see whether new or different symptoms emerge when a problem behavior is removed or altered. The evidence indicates that symptom substitution, if it does occur, certainly is not obvious. In short, there is little if any research support for this notion.)

In summary, Skinner and Freud have some things in common. The writings of both indicate: (1) an intense interest in understanding behavior, (2) an emphasis on the study of individual organisms, (3) a concern with extending their findings to social problems, (4) a belief that humans are not essentially rational, and (5) a belief in lawful, naturalistic causes of behavior. There are several differences, however, that highlight the split between radical behaviorism and psychoanalysis. Skinner was critical of Freud's (1) use of a "mental apparatus" to explain behavior, (2) distinction between conscious and unconscious states of awareness, (3) concept of defense mechanisms, and (4) assumptions regarding psychotherapy. These differences result mainly from Skinner's focus on environmental influences on behavior versus Freud's emphasis on the importance of inner emotional and mental states. Skinner (1989) made his position very clear: "Troublesome behavior is caused by troublesome contingencies of reinforcement, not by troublesome feelings or states of mind, and we can correct the trouble by correcting the contingencies" (p. 74).

S I X

Disagreements with Carl Rogers

The Humanistic Reaction

HUMANISTIC PSYCHOLOGY'S most influential figure is Carl Rogers (1902–1987). Before discussing the specific disagreements between him and Skinner, I will present a bit of background material.

The humanistic movement in psychology grew by leaps and bounds during the 1960s, partially as a reaction against both psychoanalysis and behaviorism. Abraham Maslow, one of its founders, called it the "third force" in psychology. "Humanism" or "humanistic psychology" is not easy to define precisely (distinctions could be made between these two terms, but for the purposes of this chapter they will be considered synonymous.) The psychologists who group themselves under this heading hold a variety of viewpoints, though there are also certain commonalities among them. In contrast to Skinner's emphasis on the controlling influences of environmental factors, humanists insist that the most significant determinants of human behavior are certain inner qualities such as free will and subjective experiencing. Although acknowledging that environmental factors affect us and that these factors can either enhance or inhibit our basic potentialities, humanists believe that at the core of humanness is a unique essence, a creative force, a will to grow and develop in fulfilling ways.

Though humanists are similar to Freudians in their belief that inner states are important determinants of human behavior (and can be criticized by Skinner for this in a way similar to his criticisms of Freud—see Chapter Five), they are strikingly different in their emphasis on conscious and rational decision-making processes and in their optimistic view of basic human nature (not *all* humanistic psychologists hold this optimistic view, but it *is* widespread and was held by Rogers). In general, they stress that people are essentially sociable, rational, and good, whereas Freudians tend to see strong elements of selfishness, irrationality, and destructive aggressiveness in human nature. (In the humanist sense, "rationality" typically refers to an integrated approach to life situations, in which personal feelings and other inner experiencing are combined with considerations of the external environment. It does not refer to highly intellectualized thought processes.)

Humanists often react strongly to Skinner's ideas. They consider him to have been the prime mover of a type of behaviorism that violates much of what they believe about human nature and the true meanings of human behavior. Skinner showed no respect for their concepts of free will, purposeful action, self-actualization, and inner meaning—concepts that humanists feel are vital for understanding the essence of human existence and actions. In addition, he stated explicitly his belief that humanistic psychology (along with cognitive psychology and traditional psychotherapy) is a major obstacle in psychology's path toward becoming a valuable science of behavior (Skinner, 1987b).

Skinner and Rogers: Friendly Foes

The controversy between humanists and behaviorists exists in various forms, but it is highlighted by the long-term ideological struggle between Skinner and Carl Rogers, the firmly humanistic founder of client-centered (or person-centered) therapy, advocate of encounter groups, and developer of person-centered theory. Rogers's work has been well known in psychology since the 1940s, and he is widely respected for his contributions. Rogers's humanism predated the label "humanistic psychology," but he later identified himself with that broad school of thought.

Skinner and Rogers brought a clear focus to the differences between radical behaviorism and the humanistic approach. They met in public debates and mentioned each other in their writings. Their opposition to each other's ideas was healthy and constructive, bringing out important issues for consideration. Each seemed to like the other personally. Skinner pointed out that he didn't generally engage in arguments or debates, being much more interested in simply presenting his own views, but that he made an exception in the case of his friend Carl Rogers. Rogers, despite sharp differences with many of his ideas, expressed respect for Skinner's honesty and dedication to his work.

After briefly presenting some of the major aspects of Rogers's humanistic approach, which has strongly influenced many persons in the helping professions, we will consider the specifics of the controversy between him and Skinner.

Rogers's Humanistic Approach

Rogers believed that human nature is essentially positive: basically we seek growth and fulfillment (actualization), and we want close and meaningful relations with others. He suggested that, in order for actualization to occur and for interpersonal relations to be positive and fulfilling, we must be accurately aware of our basic inner experiencing (sensations, perceptions, feelings, thoughts, and so on).

Why do so many people fail to actualize themselves? What goes wrong? Rogers explained that we have a need for *positive regard* (love and acceptance) from significant other persons in our lives, but we often receive *conditional,* rather than *unconditional,* positive regard. This means that conditions (or stipulations) are placed on the love and acceptance that we need. In simple terms, the message often received is "I will love and accept you *if* you believe or feel as I expect you to." When we get such messages directly or subtly, we are apt to yield in varying degrees to receive the positive regard that we crave—even when it means giving up what our own inner experiencing is telling us. We may deny, distort, and defend against this experiencing and convince ourselves, for example, that our sexual feelings are bad, that our occasional anger toward our parents is wrong, that creative interests must come second to "serious" pursuits, and so on. In our attempts to defend against the aspects of our inner experiencing that are considered "bad" or "wrong" (and to prevent rejection by significant others, especially during our formative years), we become more rigid, less aware of basic feelings, and less spontaneous. Our self-concepts become distorted in the direction of others' standards and values, rather than being closely related to our own deeply felt inner experiencing. In brief, this is Rogers's explanation of how we become derailed from the track toward actualization.

If we are to develop in actualizing ways, Rogers suggested that *unconditional positive regard* is necessary. That is, we need love and acceptance without conditions (or stipulations) being placed on them.* We then can remain in tune with our basic experiencing, accepting and responding to our own personal inner reactions in an open way, developing as flexible, aware, spontaneous, nondefensive persons and tending toward behaviors that are beneficial to ourselves and society. We can sense what our own real fundamental needs and wants are, while also being aware of what the surrounding environmental circumstances require. To understand Rogers's thinking, it is necessary to remember that he had an optimistic view of human nature. He believed that, if persons are allowed to develop in a warm, accepting atmosphere, they will not only actualize themselves but will also live and work more harmoniously with others.

In *client-centered* (or *person-centered*) *therapy,* which Rogers developed, the therapist attempts to create interpersonal conditions that will allow clients to regain contact with their basic inner experiencing. The three major attitudes that client-centered therapists try to maximize are: (1) *empathic understanding,* (2) *unconditional positive regard,* and (3) *genuineness.* If the therapist can sense empathically the subjective meanings that experiences have for the client and

---

*The concept of *unconditional positive regard* is different from Skinner's concept of *positive reinforcement.* The idea behind unconditional positive regard is that, if a person is completely accepted for what he or she is, the person will develop in positive ways; again, Rogers's positive view of basic human nature is important if this concept is to be assumed workable. Skinner made no assumptions about human nature being either positive or negative; therefore he suggested that positive reinforcement be used to shape and maintain desirable and constructive behaviors.

reflect this understanding, the client can gain clearer perspectives on these experiences. By accepting and caring for the client unconditionally, the therapist presumably helps the client to become more self-accepting, allowing a fuller range of thoughts, feelings, perceptions, and sensations into awareness without self-condemnation. By being genuine or "real," the therapist maintains an honest interaction with the client, dropping the pretenses and false facades that often prevail in everyday life. If these three therapist attitudes—empathy, unconditional positive regard, and genuineness—can be maintained with reasonable consistency, Rogers believed that clients will grasp the essential meanings of their own inner experiencing and beneficial behavioral changes will result.

In Rogers's view, each of us has within us the resources to actualize our true selves, and these resources are mobilized if adequate conditions are provided. Client-centered therapists claim considerable success with their clients. Despite these successes, however, there is not sufficient evidence to state conclusively that Rogers' *interpretation* of why clients improve during therapy is correct.

The Rogers-Skinner Controversy

Skinner has been critical of Rogers's assumptions about what occurs during therapy. Client-centered therapy emphasizes the client's responsibility for getting better. Though the therapist sets the conditions of empathy, unconditional positive regard, and genuineness, it is the client who must get in touch with inner experiencing and choose how to live. Skinner suggested that the notions of the client looking within and making free choices about what to do are irrelevant. In his view there are no answers deep within the person. People are always controlled in one way or another, and the goal should be to free them from *aversive* control. They often need assistance in developing different, more effective behaviors and in finding new sources of positive reinforcement, but there is no such thing as free choice based on inner experiencing. According to Skinner, free choice is an illusion.

Skinner implied that client-centered therapists do control patients in various ways, even when such control is denied. With subtle verbal statements and physical gestures (for example, nodding the head at particular times), client-centered therapists may inadvertently shape certain behaviors in their clients. Skinner indicated that, if a client-centered therapist actually is successful in maintaining a completely nonjudgmental stance, the client's behaviors then will be controlled by forces outside the therapy situation, such as the reactions of others and earlier religious or ethical training. The effects of these outside influences may change because of aspects of the therapy experience; for example, the client may become more assertive with others because he or she is being encouraged subtly by the therapist to talk about feelings and to "be honest." In Skinner's view, any changes that occur in the client's behaviors are due to such environmental events and *not* to changes in inner states such as the self-concept.

Skinner's thoroughgoing emphasis on objective behavioral determinants and Rogers's persistent belief that inner, subjective experiencing is basic and essential formed the basis of other disagreements between the two psychologists. Rogers suggested that, in addition to the objective research of behaviorists, it is important to try to grasp subjectively what persons are experiencing within. This is a *phenomenological approach.* He believed that an important influence on individuals is their immediate, conscious experiencing of themselves and of the world around them and that, if persons are to be understood fully, we must be able to view reality through their eyes. In short, a person's subjective view of reality is important in determining how he or she will act. For example, the same barking dog may affect two people differently because of their different subjective perceptions of the situation. One person may walk over and pet the dog, whereas the other person may run away. In Rogers's view, if we are to understand these two different reactions, we must understand how each person perceives the barking dog.

Skinner reacted to such suggestions by pointing out that we can't gain direct knowledge of another person's inner experiencing. We don't have immediate access to these inner processes, and it is futile to try to build scientific knowledge on inferences about subjective states. Rather, we must stick to objective approaches and look for functional relationships between observable events and observable behaviors. For instance, in the preceding example, there is no reason to assume that the two persons react differently to a barking dog because of different "subjective perceptions." A Skinnerian analysis suggests that they have had different experiences with dogs. These experiences, reinforcing or punishing, can be considered the critical factors determining approach or avoidance behaviors. Skinner believed that, by considering internal states (such as subjective perceptions) as causes of behavior, the environmental determinants tend to be underemphasized or overlooked (Skinner similarly criticized Freud's speculations about inner states—see Chapter Five).

Another difference of opinion between Rogers and Skinner involved educational practices. Rogers believed that learning should occur in a relatively unstructured setting in which resources are available to the learner so that he or she can pursue personal interests. In his view, people are naturally curious; if they are free to follow their own chosen paths of learning, they will educate themselves. He felt that self-guided learning should be the crux of education. The schools should trust students to follow their own leads and allow for emotional, as well as intellectual, learning. He referred to this approach as educating the "whole person."

It is interesting that both Rogers and Skinner were very critical of the existing educational system and recommended drastic changes. Rogers advocated less structure and more freedom for students—education should be student centered. On the other side, Skinner advocated *more* structure, but of a different type than now exists. For example, he strongly opposed the use of aversive control to promote learning. He believed that too often students are exposed to threats of punishment (poor grades, reprimands, failure, and so on) as a means of getting them to work hard. In his view, education should be based on positive reinforcement. Students should be given material in sufficiently small units so that each unit can be mastered, and the student's progress should be reinforced before the next unit is undertaken. In this way, effective learning takes place, and the student's feelings about the experience are positive (Skinner said that positive reinforcement results in good feelings). To say that Skinner advocated more structured education means that he favored carefully planned, systematic presentations of material with ample opportunities for the learner's progress to be reinforced (programmed material and teaching machines are helpful in this regard).

Skinner suggested that his educational goals were in agreement with those of Rogers, even though they differed on how to achieve those goals. They both wanted people to feel positive about their educational experiences and to develop independence. (Also, they both were very optimistic about the potential of humans to learn, given adequate conditions.) By "independence" Skinner meant that persons should be able to act without having to be told what to do and when to do it. Also, he wanted people to *feel* free even though they actually can never *be* free from the effects of environmental factors; independence and feelings of freedom come from building a rich repertoire of behaviors based on positive reinforcement and from situations in which aversive control is absent. He believed that Rogers's reliance on inner determinants to motivate and guide learning was misplaced and suggested that "motivation" and "inner guidance" do not emerge from somewhere within the person. Rather, behaviors that suggest these qualities result from appropriate reinforcements.

The suggestions of both Rogers and Skinner have been applied in various educational settings with claims of considerable success. Who, then, is right? At this point there is no conclusive answer. There are so many different types of subject matter, student abilities and backgrounds, educational situations, and other relevant factors that it is premature to judge one approach as being most effective overall. Also, there may be certain common elements of learning situations that produce good outcomes. For example, when Skinner's systematic, structured approach is used, a certain amount of general "warmth and acceptance" on the part of the instructor may be important (Skinner might have agreed with this but perhaps would have added that "warmth and acceptance" should be defined in terms of specific instructor behaviors and their effects). When Rogers's approach is to be used, it is likely that certain basic skills can be taught most efficiently with a systematic approach, before allowing students "to pursue their own interests" (Rogers probably would have agreed with this but would have added that it is always important for students to want to learn the material, however basic it is). In short, it doesn't seem that the two approaches are necessarily mutually exclusive. However, the larger behaviorist-humanist educational dispute focuses on the issue of the importance of outer versus inner determinants of learning.

Rogers's belief that human nature essentially is positive ties in with his educational beliefs. He felt that there is a potential for growth within each person that needs to be released. Skinner, on the other hand, suggested that the positive forces assumed to lie deep within our personalities are simply the things that we can accomplish with appropriate reinforcement. These different perspectives on human nature affect educational perspectives. For Rogers, freedom to develop inner resources was foremost, which leads to "open classrooms" and other unstructured settings. For Skinner, the planning of environmental conditions was foremost, which leads to systematic applications of positive reinforcement in the classroom and to the use of programmed material and teaching machines.

At a 1956 symposium featuring an exchange between Rogers and Skinner, Rogers indicated that he believed "the major flaw" in the type of behavioral control advocated by Skinner "is the denial, misunderstanding, or gross underestimation of the place of ends, goals, or values in their relationship to science" (Rogers & Skinner, 1956, p. 1061). This comment brings out yet another aspect of the controversy between these two men. Rogers went on to explain that there is always a "prior subjective choice" about the purposes of scientific work, once again pointing out what he considered an essential part of all human pursuits: inner subjective experiencing. In his opinion, even the most objective behavioral scientist must make certain value decisions that are outside of science itself. In other words, the scientist must decide what to study, how to study it, and how to use the data obtained, and these decisions arise from the inner experiencing of the scientist. For Rogers, the initial decision to be objective and scientific cannot itself be derived from science; rather, it is a subjectively chosen value.

In response to Rogers's statements about the significance of subjective value choices, Skinner indicated that these choices are really determined by reinforcement. Some behavioral outcomes are reinforcing, and others aren't. People "choose" or "decide" to do that which is reinforcing. Expanding on Skinner's reasoning, it can be said that the scientist's behaviors, and accompanying "values," also are controlled by reinforcers, rather than by some inner choice that he or she makes to engage in scientific pursuits. If the background of a scientist was known in detail, it would very likely show a shaping process that led the scientist to use certain techniques and to study certain phenomena. Simply stated, scientists do what they do (and hold certain scientific values) because their science-related behaviors have been reinforced, perhaps by parents and teachers initially, and later by colleagues. Also, the fact that an experiment produces results may be reinforcing in and of itself. (Skinner suggested that his own productive scientific career was influenced by a fortunate personal history of reinforcement for such efforts.) Considering the possible influences of reinforcers on the scientist's behavior, is it still necessary to say that he or she "chooses" to do research? The answer to this question depends on whether you are a humanist or a behaviorist. The humanist insists that choice enters into the process, whereas the behaviorist maintains that the notion of choice is irrelevant.

To conclude this section, let's briefly consider the differences between Rogers and Skinner on the issue of broad social change. Rogers's writings indicate that he favored opening up society's institutions; they should be more responsive to innovations and more geared toward change based on the needs of individuals for growth and fulfillment. He felt that society is too static. Rigid rules and codes of expected conduct stifle the creative development of mature, actualized individuals. Rogers was perhaps most vocal about the restricting influences of two of our most revered social institutions: education and the family. He felt that they exert too much inhibiting control over persons and need to change in the direction of fostering freedom and actualization.

The most basic difference between Rogers's and Skinner's views on society involves the issue of control. Rogers believed that we need much less of it. Skinner believed that we must have it, but in a different form than exists presently. Skinner indicated that behavioral engineering—the systematic application of behavioral procedures—is essential for an effective society. The type of control that Skinner recommended is based on positive reinforcement. People should behave in productive and creative ways because society positively reinforces such behaviors. In other words, the extensive use of punishment and aversive control by social institutions must be replaced by positive forms of control. This is the general formula offered by Skinner for social change (other recommendations will be discussed in Chapter Seven). Both he and Rogers were adamant about the need for social change, but they differed on the question of how to bring about the desired outcomes.

It is interesting to consider what makes a person a humanist or a behaviorist. Rogers would have said that it is mainly a matter of choice, whereas Skinner would have said that it depends strongly on the individual's history of reinforcement. Basically, this implies that Rogers (from his perspective) made a subjective decision to be a humanist, whereas Skinner (from his perspective) was conditioned by environmental factors to be a behaviorist. Regardless of the determining factors, humanists and behaviorists differ in their basic assumptions, in the terminology they use to describe and explain human functioning, in the kinds of research they do, in their therapeutic techniques, in their educational procedures, and in their prescriptions for social change. The humanist-behaviorist controversy isn't likely to subside quickly. The issues involved are significant and complex and very difficult (perhaps even impossible) to resolve completely.

SEVEN

Relevance for Today's World

SKINNER ADDRESSED contemporary social problems in a number of ways. As indicated in the preceding chapter, he suggested changes in our educational system and in other social institutions. His novel, *Walden Two,* shows how behavioral concepts might be applied in a small community, and his later book *Beyond Freedom and Dignity* deals with the broad question of the survival of the culture and society's need for behavioral technology. Also, he wrote articles and gave lectures on these topics. With regard to practical applications of Skinner's behavioral procedures, many therapists, psychologists, teachers, business and industrial supervisors, parents, and others have used them effectively in a variety of real-life situations. That fact alone is evidence that Skinner's psychology is relevant for today's world.

In this chapter more of Skinner's concerns about our society and its directions will be discussed. However, I won't cover many of the specific procedures that constitute the growing field of behavior modification, which involves practical applications of the behavioral concepts of Skinner and others (to clarify again, "behavior modification" is a general label that includes operant procedures as well as other approaches; Skinner preferred the phrase "applied behavior analysis" to refer specifically to practical experimental applications of the concepts developed by him and his colleagues). There are a number of books that treat the specifics of current work in behavior modification (for example, Kazdin, 1989; Martin & Pear, 1988; Watson & Tharp, 1989), and these works should be consulted by those who are interested. Also, the *Journal of Applied Behavior Analysis* is devoted to articles on practical experimental applications of operant procedures and is a primary source of information.

Walden Two

When Skinner wrote *Walden Two* in 1945 (it was published three years later), he was attempting to show the possibilities of applying behavioral concepts derived from laboratory research to the running of a small community. (He estimated the size of the town as 1000 but indicated that the best number might be different; the most effective size needs to be determined through experimentation.) The book sold slowly for a number of years but then began an upward trend that reached over 2 million copies by 1982—and it's still selling.

Skinner said that, when he wrote *Walden Two,* he was guessing how his experimental results could be applied. At that time almost nothing had been done to test these findings in practical human situations. Today, however, much less guessing is necessary. The growth in applied behavior analysis, especially during the 1960s and since, has provided considerable evidence that human behavior can be affected beneficially by applying laboratory-derived procedures. This has been shown in "normal" situations such as schools and businesses, as well as in institutions that care for retarded persons, individuals with psychotic disorders, and other persons with special problems. This evidence allows greater confidence in tho possibilities for planned communities based on behavioral technology.

Although there have been no experimental communities exactly like the fictional *Walden Two,* the general model provided by Skinner has served as an inspiration. The oldest example is Twin Oaks, near Louisa, Virginia. It was begun in 1967 by eight people and evolved over the years as the membership and community practices changed; by 1984 there were 78 members, and humanistic, as well as behavioristic, practices had been adopted (Cordes, 1984, p. 1).

Kathleen Kinkade, one of the original members, wrote a book describing the community (*A Walden Two Experiment: The First Five Years of Twin Oaks Community,* published by William Morrow and Company, 1973). In a foreword to this book, Skinner pointed out that, even though the development of Twin Oaks was not identical to what he proposed in *Walden Two,* it was a valuable test of the application of certain fundamental ideas and provided interesting information. He believed that experimental communities have to cope with problems that are similar to those the world is facing. Therefore the outcomes of these attempts are relevant to larger issues.

Los Horcones, Mexico, is another example of a small community inspired by Skinner. It was founded in 1973 by six adults and one child. By 1989 the membership was 28 adults and 11 children. They are sustained by farming and by providing educational programs for children outside the community. There is a detailed code of behavior, clothes and other items are shared, cooperation and equality are stressed, and positive reinforcement is used systematically to get children to master increasingly complex topics in the classroom. One of the founders has been quoted as saying: "The central point is that we use the science of behaviorism . . . to design a collective environment" (Rohter, 1989, p. C1). Los Horcones, Skinner suggested, comes closest among the communities inspired by *Walden Two* to adhering to his concepts.

Some of Skinner's advice about important aspects of community life, as expressed in *Walden Two* and other writings, is as follows: (1) *Childrearing* should be communal, so that the security and training of children doesn't depend solely on the presence and abilities of biological parents. Specialists should have primary responsibility for the day-to-day care of children, thereby preventing problems caused by inexperience, inconsistent demands, abuse, overprotection, and other shortcomings of modern family life. (2) *Education* should be related to practical situations within the community, so that students see concrete applications of the subject matter. Additional provisions, such as specialized books and other materials, should be made for those who want to pursue particular interests. Programmed materials and teaching machines should be used more extensively. (3) *Work* should be productive, with everyone expected to contribute a modest amount of effort. The emphasis within the community should be on a simple but satisfying life; there should be no need for long hours of work to provide useless services or goods. (4) *Leisure time* should be ample, and activities should center on doing rather than merely observing. (5) *Personal relations* should be noncompetitive and intimate, making it more likely that people will be friendly and affectionate toward one another. Intimacy among community members also is important because it allows immediate approval of desirable behaviors and censure of undesirable behaviors. In other words, the impersonal situations that characterize much of contemporary society should be avoided. (6) *Sex roles* should not be structured along traditional lines; rather, both men and women should pursue whatever work or leisure activities fit their abilities. Childrearing should not be solely the women's responsibility. (7) *Young people and old people* should have active roles in community life. The young should be allowed to assume a full role earlier, including work and marriage, and the old should be able to contribute longer. (8) *Psychotics or retarded persons and others with special problems* should be cared for within the community, and some useful role should be found for them whenever possible. Behavior-modification procedures are often effective with these persons, allowing them to perform useful tasks and to enjoy certain leisure activities. (9) *Government* operates best when people behave responsibly toward one another. In fact, when people in a community have a face-to-face familiarity with one another and interact in cooperative and reinforcing ways, there is very little need for governmental regulations.

In order to accomplish the above, Skinner suggested that "smaller would be better" with regard to our living circumstances. It is easier to apply behavioral procedures in small communities than in major population areas or in large, complex organizations. Small communities provide the advantages of close interpersonal contacts. Also, if important reinforcers (productive work, contacts with friends, leisure activities, and so on) are available *within* the community, there is less need for traveling and therefore less wasted time and resources. In short, Skinner believed that it would be more efficient, and easier to plan and manage things, if people were decentralized and lived in small towns. He saw a network of communities like Walden Two as a constructive alternative to our present system.

An essential feature of the small communities visualized by Skinner is that they be "experimental." This means that the results of each social change should be monitored closely to see that they are beneficial to individuals and to the community. (This approach is similar to that used in scientific laboratories, where the researcher varies some condition in order to study the effects.) This method of systematically instituting changes and carefully checking the results allows corrections to be made before undesirable outcomes multiply. Again, it is a matter of paying attention to the consequences of actions, something that Skinner emphasized consistently. In his opinion, we do far too little of it. We often make changes and *assume* that certain outcomes occur without collecting data or making careful observations to back up our assumptions. If Skinner's advice were followed, we would behave more like scientists when planning and managing our lives and the communities within which we live.

Fundamentally, what Skinner advocated was a cultural revolution. He believed that major changes must be made in our overcrowded, overconsuming, and impersonal society. Our survival, he suggested, may well depend on these changes. His answer to our social problems doesn't rely on political action or governmental regulations. Rather, what is needed is the application of behavioral-science findings to our everyday lives, as well as the collection of more information about the effects of environmental conditions on behavior.

Beyond Freedom and Dignity

Skinner's 1971 book, *Beyond Freedom and Dignity,* expresses themes similar to some of those in *Walden Two.* However, it isn't a work of fiction; rather, it is a treatise on the need for behavioral technology (or behavioral engineering) in today's society and on the problems involved in establishing such a technology. In earlier chapters we covered a number of points that are related to Skinner's ideas in *Beyond Freedom and Dignity,* but now we'll look directly at several major issues discussed in that book. Again, I'll try to present Skinner's ideas as simply as possible, and I'll provide some of my own elaborations and examples. For fuller details on his views, *Beyond Freedom and Dignity* should be consulted.

Skinner suggested that, although enormous advances have been made in fields such as biology and physics, allowing sophisticated technologies to be developed with regard to contraception, weapons systems, agriculture, medicine, and so on, there has been relatively little progress in the development of a technology of behavior. A science of human behavior upon which such a technology could be based has been slow to emerge, and therefore governmental, educational, economic, and other social institutions continue to plod along, showing little improvement over the years.

As mentioned at the beginning of this chapter, there has been considerable use of behavioral techniques based on the concepts of Skinner and his colleagues. However, Skinner believed that widespread resistance remains to advances in this approach to individual and social problems. This resistance prevents us from moving with sufficient speed toward the broader development and use of behavioral technology, and our society suffers severely from ever-increasing difficulties as a result. He expressed considerable doubt about our continued ability to maintain a viable and strong society unless we take more seriously the role of a science of human behavior.

Why is it that, while other sciences have shown dramatic progress, behavioral science has lagged behind? According to Skinner, the major reason is that we look for the causes of behavior in the wrong place. We tend to look for internal causes, residing within individuals: intentions, purposes, decisions, aims, values, plans, and so on commonly are considered the moving forces behind our actions. Feelings and states of mind are emphasized in explaining why people behave as they do. We give relatively little attention to the antecedents and consequences of behavior, and Skinner believed that it is these environmental conditions that provide the details upon which a science of behavior must be built.

Why do we continue to insist on inner motivators of behavior, rather than taking a more thorough look at environmental causes? Two important reasons suggested by Skinner are: (1) since we do have feelings, often strong and immediate ones, they seem to us to cause our behaviors, and (2) environmental influences on behavior often are subtle and difficult to observe, and therefore they easily go unnoticed.

It is easy to understand why feelings seem to cause behavior. They exist immediately within us, are often intense, and accompany our actions. It would be surprising if we *didn't* believe they caused our behaviors. In Skinner's view, however, they are "by-products" of the same environmental conditions that influence how we behave. To give a couple of simple examples (similar to ones given earlier in this book): If your behavior is reinforced with praise or approval, you not only are more likely to behave similarly again, but you also are likely to "feel good." In other words, positive reinforcement has affected both your behavior and your feelings. In another case your behavior might be punished. You then would not be likely to repeat it immediately, and you would probably feel guilt, resentment, anger, or some other emotion, depending on the circumstances. The important point made by Skinner is that "feeling good" or "feeling guilty" is not what causes your behaviors. These feelings are controlled by environmental events such as reinforcements and punishments, just as overt behaviors are controlled by these consequences.

Environmental influences on behavior often aren't obvious and therefore don't provide a clear alternative explanation. The effects of the environment often are misunderstood. Skinner explained that the environment doesn't primarily push or pull us around; rather, it *selects* certain behaviors because of their consequences. A behavior is *selected* (becomes more likely to occur) if it is reinforced. We emit many different types of responses during our lifetimes, but only some of them become part of our regular behavior patterns. Those that do are the ones that have reinforcing consequences (they are either positively or negatively reinforced—see Chapter Two for more details). The selective nature of the environment often operates inconspicuously; it doesn't "stand out" with dramatic force as do our feelings. Therefore, much of the determining action of the environment (including both physical and social influences) goes unnoticed while we focus on the more obvious feelings that we have or that others express. (Skinner drew a parallel between Darwin's theory of evolution and his own ideas. Evolutionary theory emphasized the selective nature of the environment with regard to *genetic* characteristics of the species, and Skinner emphasized the selective nature of the environment with regard to *behavioral* characteristics that develop during an individual's lifetime.)

The results of realizing that the environment *selects* behaviors because of their consequences are: (1) explanations based on feelings and other inner states are abandoned in favor of the careful examination of environmental conditions; and (2) behavioral changes are brought about by changing the environmental conditions to which individuals are exposed. Skinner pointed out that he and his colleagues proceeded along these lines and made significant advances in developing a science of behavior. What stands in the way of greater use of this science are certain traditional practices that are prevalent in our society and pervade our legal, economic, and educational systems, as well as other social institutions.

The practices that are especially opposed to the development and use of behavioral technology have to do with individual autonomy: the *freedom* of each person to choose or decide his or her own course of action and the *dignity* (or worth) that is awarded the person who successfully overcomes obstacles or achieves admirable goals. The controversy that arises from challenges to freedom and dignity gets in the way of an objective appraisal of the benefits of a technology of behavior.

The title of his book, *Beyond Freedom and Dignity,* indicates the central issue that Skinner believed is involved in the adoption of a behavioral-technology approach to solving society's problems. He suggested that we must move beyond the traditional concepts of *freedom* and *dignity* and stop acting in terms of individual autonomy. We must investigate and develop environmental conditions that will reduce overpopulation, disease, pollution, and other social ills while promoting health, peace, conservation of natural resources, and other socially beneficial goals. As long as people are seen as autonomous beings who have the *freedom* to decide their own fates and whose *dignity* or worth depends on admirable actions arising from their personal inner qualities, we will not focus sufficiently on the controlling influences of the environment, especially the antecedents and consequences of behaviors. Therefore we will miss opportunities to develop a stronger and better society by improving the conditions that affect our behaviors.

In discussing the details of "freedom," Skinner suggested that commonly it is seen as a state of mind or a feeling and that humans generally are considered to have a will to be free. Therefore there is an emphasis on the need to throw off aversive control so that the individual can be free to live life on his or her own terms. Unfortunately, this line of reasoning easily leads to the conclusion that *all* control is wrong; the possibility of controlling social conditions for beneficial results tends to be either ignored or actively rejected. In Skinner's view, not only should we try to free persons from aversive control (which is what the advocates of freedom recommend), but we should take the next step and create controls that produce positive outcomes. If we remain fixed on the notion that freedom is threatened by *all* forms of control, we lose the advantages that behavioral technology can provide.

The traditional concept of "dignity," which involves worthiness bestowed on individuals when they are given credit for admirable behaviors, also is threatened by behavioral technology. In Skinner's approach, all behavior is determined by genetic and environmental factors, and there are no "admirable behaviors" arising out of the depths of one's special "inner character" or "personality." In other words, what we do (admirable or not) was viewed by Skinner as the result of conditions (genetic and environmental) that we have no part in "deciding upon" or "choosing"; therefore, credit giving is inappropriate when it implies that the person has acted autonomously. We are so used to giving credit to, and honoring, individuals for their achievements, and to seeking credit and honor for ourselves, that Skinner's suggestions are likely to seem alien to us.

In cases when credit is given or taken for accomplishments, the causes of these accomplishments are not readily observable. There are many examples of heroic, artistic, inventive, persevering, and other "admirable" behaviors in which the only available explanation seems to be that there is some special inner quality of the hero, the artist, the inventor, or the hardworking individual. Behavioral science, as advocated by Skinner, involves the examination of how these types of behaviors (as well as "ordinary" behaviors) come about through environmental influences. His assumption was that environmental circumstances, however subtle or inconspicuous, *are* influential. Once the relevant environmental conditions are discovered, this knowledge can then be used to promote further socially beneficial accomplishments. A problem emerges, however, when we balk at this approach because it seems to reduce our dignity.

Skinner suggested that we don't really want to discover the external circumstances that control our "admirable" behaviors because we no longer would be able to "take credit" for them—our "worth," *as we presently conceive it,* would be reduced. This situation blocks the maximum development and use of environmental controls that could lead to greater human accomplishments.

In *Beyond Freedom and Dignity,* Skinner took up another issue that he discussed in many other publications, including *Walden Two:* the role of punishment in society. He again pointed out that we frequently control and are controlled by punitive means, such as actual or threatened censure, ridicule, criticism, or physical harm. Social institutions such as those of government and religion, as well as individuals, often use punishment (or threatened punishment) as a way of suppressing unwanted behaviors.

Though punishment may be effective on an immediate basis and may continue to suppress behavior if the punisher remains present (or if the punishment was of sufficient intensity), Skinner indicated that it fails in the long run. It doesn't actually eliminate tendencies to behave in punishable ways. Also, as was mentioned earlier, the use of punishment may result in escape or avoidance behaviors. Individuals who are punished or threatened with punishment are likely to find ways of getting away from the punishing circumstances: schoolchildren may cut classes, workers may quit or feign illnesses, wives or husbands may desert their spouses, and so on.

Another good example of what Skinner is talking about are laws that rely on punitive measures and aversive control for their effectiveness. Speed limits, for example, are maintained primarily by the tickets given to those who speed, by the threat of receiving a ticket, by the presence of police, or by indications that speed-monitoring equipment is being used. In the absence of these conditions many individuals exceed the speed limit. Also, in order to avoid the punishment of receiving a ticket, drivers use devices such as radar detectors.

Following Skinner's approach, perhaps another system for maintaining speed limits should be introduced that provides positive reinforcement for slower driving. It might sound farfetched, but maybe the main purpose of highway police should be to notice good driving and to signal their approval (instead of the reprimand or speeding ticket that usually follows being noticed by the police). Additionally, letters of praise could be sent (although the effectiveness of this reinforcer might be limited because it is not immediate; reinforcers are most effective when they immediately follow the appropriate behavior). Another possibility would be to put gas-mileage markings on the speedometer, so that driving at reasonable speeds would be reinforced immediately by the indication that good gas mileage was being obtained.

Returning to Skinner's views on punishment, he suggested that it is possible to construct a society in which punishable behaviors occur infrequently or never. In other words, if behavioral technology was used to control behavior in nonpunitive ways, good behaviors would be common, and there would be little need for punitive techniques. This suggestion, Skinner indicated, is not easily accepted by those who advocate freedom of choice and who accept the traditional concept of human dignity based on individual, autonomous control of one's own achievements. In simple terms, the objections are that, if a person's good behavior is determined by environmental control, what happens to his or her freedom to choose to be good, and how can credit be given for behaving well?

Again, the concept of individual autonomy enters the picture and actually supports (in an indirect way) the retention of punitive measures. In a punitive society, if persons are good, it seems to be because they have chosen to be good, and therefore they deserve credit. It's like saying: "If you don't take personal responsibility for yourself and don't control yourself in the appropriate ways, you will be punished. You have the choice. It's up to you. If you decide to behave well, you will be showing strong character and you will deserve to be admired." Skinner believed that this is a relatively ineffective way to get people to behave well (as is obvious just by looking at all of the undesirable behaviors that exist). However, it does allow the advocates of freedom and dignity to feel comfortable, because individuals appear to have the freedom to decide whether or not they will do the correct thing; credit can then be given to those who "make the proper decisions." If an effective and nonpunitive behavioral technology was introduced and people behaved well because of planned environmental conditions, there would be no "personal responsibility" for good behavior, no "freedom" to choose to behave well, and no "dignity" bestowed on individuals for their achievements.

Of course, that doesn't mean that *feelings* of responsibility, freedom, and dignity would be eliminated. It simply means that the traditional reliance upon these concepts, which now dominate society, would be replaced with behavioral-technology procedures. As Skinner pointed out time and again, the basic approach of his behavioral technology is positive reinforcement. This was his preferred means of controlling behavior, and it is not only effective in getting people to behave well, but it also makes them feel good.

Skinner believed that his own behavior was controlled primarily by his environment. He didn't see himself as an exception to the rules of his psychology. Despite the fact that he was controlled by environmental conditions (for example, the reinforcing consequences of his research and writing behaviors), he said that he felt free. This feeling of freedom did not depend on *actually* being free (Skinner said there is no such thing); it came from a positively reinforcing environment. So, in a Skinnerian society using behavioral technology, people would still be able to feel free, worthy, and responsible, even though their behaviors were being controlled. (An important point: Skinner believed that we *presently* are controlled by our environments and that there is no way to escape being controlled; the goal, then, in his view, is to construct nonpunitive and maximally effective environmental conditions that will promote individual and social improvements—and good feelings.)

In a society that relies heavily on punitive techniques to control individuals, much time and effort are wasted as people attempt to escape or avoid punishing consequences (and, of course, these punitive techniques also produce negative feelings in those being controlled). This weakens the society; a stronger society is likely when positive reinforcement is used systematically to shape and maintain productive and beneficial activities.

In our society, despite the high incidence of punitive control, there obviously are numerous successful persons who "develop their potential" and contribute to society. But should we be satisfied with this? Also, are there countertrends, such as delinquency, crime, unemployment, pollution, and wasted resources, that need correcting before they cause the downfall of society? Skinner's behavioral-technology suggestions are directed at improving the functioning of society through a more systematic and scientifically based approach. In other words, his plan leaves less to chance. Though some fortunate individuals presently are exposed to favorable environmental conditions, Skinner raised the possibility of making such exposure more common. If he is correct, and if his plan was adopted on a wide scale, it could mobilize human potential far beyond present hopes.

In addressing the issue of whether or not our culture will survive in the long run, Skinner pointed out the importance of inducing individuals to work for its survival. Expressing a familiar theme, he suggested that we can't rely on wise judgments, feelings of concern, or other mental or emotional states to save us. Rather, positive thoughts, enthusiastic feelings, *and* (most importantly) culture-saving behaviors all depend on the ways in which the culture provides positive and negative reinforcers, and the emphasis is best placed on positive reinforcement.

In *Walden Two,* Skinner presented his ideas for a utopian society based on behavioral-science findings. It is a fictional community in which childrearing, work, leisure, and other important human activities are controlled beneficially by the manipulation of environmental conditions. In *Beyond Freedom and Dignity,* Skinner's main point is that the traditional practices of freedom and dignity, which emphasize doing away with all forms of external control, prevent the maximum development of behavioral science and the use of behavioral technology. The advocates of freedom and dignity, in his view, are so involved in suppressing punitive control that they fail to see the benefits of constructive environmental control. According to Skinner, it is a fact that all of us are controlled all of the time. Therefore, it would be better if we designed positive controls to replace those that are aversive or punitive and to shape behaviors that would help ensure the survival of our culture.

The points mentioned so far in this chapter certainly do not cover all that Skinner said about contemporary society; only some highlights have been presented. In both *Walden Two* and *Beyond Freedom and Dignity,* as well as in other writings, he discussed additional issues, some of which are too involved to go into here. However, to expand somewhat on Skinner's concerns about society and contemporary issues, a few more topics will be covered.

Education

Some of Skinner's ideas about education and the advantages of using programmed instruction and teaching machines were discussed in Chapters Two and Four. To cover thoroughly the implications of Skinner's psychology for the field of education would involve applying the full range of his concepts: reinforcement, rule-governed and contingency-shaped behaviors, chaining, discrimination training, and so on. In a sense, almost *all* of his ideas are relevant to education. Here, however, the primary focus will be on his view of effective teaching in terms of *priming, prompting,* and *vanishing* (a magician's word that Skinner borrowed).

Priming is getting someone to behave in a certain way for the first time, so that the behavior can be reinforced. This can be done by showing or telling the person how to behave. He or she is likely to do as shown or told if the teacher is "trusted," which means that imitating behavior or following instructions was reinforced in the past.

Once behavior has been primed and reinforced initially, *prompting* may be necessary until the behavior has been strengthened sufficiently by further reinforcement. This involves supplying some part of the behavior, or some cue or hint, that enables the learner to continue; for example, teachers may prompt students by giving part of an answer, enabling them to complete it. When the behavior is sufficiently strong, *vanishing* (or removing the prompts) is important. At this point the student should be able to behave "independently."

Effective teaching, then, involves the priming and prompting of behavior that is reinforced immediately; the behavior is thereby strengthened, and the prompts can be withdrawn. It sounds easy, doesn't it? In the average classroom, however, it is very difficult. Consider teachers who have 20 to 30 students or more. How do they manage to prime, prompt, and reinforce immediately each student's behavior? In addition, how do they present material progressively so that each student moves along at her or his own pace? The task generally is overwhelming.

The solution to this educational problem, according to Skinner, can be found in the use of teaching machines. He likened computerized teaching, with programmed material, to instruction by a tutor. Priming, prompting, and immediate reinforcement, with eventual vanishing, can be provided on an individual basis, something that teachers faced with large numbers of students cannot do. Additionally, with programmed instruction the only limit on what a student can learn is the availability of programs (students are not limited by their teacher's range of knowledge). The teacher has more time to get to know students and to serve as a counselor.

Skinner (1984) believed that an important aspect of "the shame of American education" is that programmed instruction is rarely used in schools (he pointed out that it is used much more widely in industry). Theories of education that stress vague ideas such as "improving cognitive deficits," "inspiring critical thinking," and "increasing self-esteem" (from a Skinnerian perspective, it is learning that increases self-esteem, not self-esteem that increases learning), and whose proponents label behavioristic proposals as "simplistic," "dehumanizing," and "asocial," are among the obstacles that Skinner saw as blocking the adoption of a technology of teaching that includes programmed instruction. He urged schools of education to change their emphasis and to train teachers to use that technology.

To continue a bit further with priming, prompting, and vanishing, Skinner indicated that verbal behavior can be taught using this procedure (which is similar to shaping, discussed in Chapter Two). For example, suppose you want to teach a very young child to use the word "cup." You hold it up and say "cup" (priming the response) and then praise (reinforce) any response that approximates the word. After this has occurred several times, you then point to the cup and make the beginning sound (prompting the response) and again reinforce the child's appropriate behavior. Eventually it is no longer necessary to give any hints (the prompts can be vanished). The contingencies of reinforcement that result in the acquisition of a language by a child generally do not occur this systematically or precisely, so learning to talk is a relatively slow process. (In my opinion, parents sometimes try too hard to speed up this process with excessive use of procedures similar to those being discussed. It's probably better to prime, prompt, reinforce, and vanish without "putting on pressure.")

Let's consider one more application of these concepts. Think about traditional lecture-discussion courses in high schools and colleges. As already indicated, Skinner suggested that it is very difficult to maximize teaching effectiveness in large classes unless programmed instruction is used. However, there are some traditional courses in which a number of students do learn quite well, and I believe that Skinner's concepts help to explain how this occurs. When instructors present important information in clear and interesting ways, they are more likely to *prime* the appropriate student behaviors of talking and writing accurately about the subject matter. Accurate student responses in class discussions and on exams are *prompted* by supplying part of the information and allowing students to supply the rest. Students' accurate responses are reinforced as quickly as possible by the instructor's favorable comments, by good exam grades, and by being correct. If this process is successful, the student leaves the course with a richer behavioral repertoire (he or she "knows more"); prompts have been *vanished,* and the student behaves "independently."

The preceding might be considered an ideal scenario for a traditionally taught course, and sometimes such courses do go well. At other times, for a variety of reasons, the process breaks down. For example, conditions external to the course (too many other activities, poor health, relationship problems, financial difficulties, and so on) may disrupt or suppress the instructor's appropriate behaviors and reduce his or her effectiveness; it's also possible that the appropriate teaching behaviors were never learned. In addition, there is the constant problem of pacing the presentation of material so that all of the students keep up and none get bored; I've found this to be the major difficulty when teaching large lecture-discussion courses; here, of course, is where teaching machines and programmed instruction have a strong advantage.

Regardless of the teaching method used, an important consideration in education should be whether the behaviors acquired will be useful beyond the classroom. In Skinner's terms, this depends in large part on whether the behaviors will be reinforced in the real world. Students are likely to become disillusioned, depressed, or angry when they find that what they've learned is not applicable— perhaps they can't get a job, or their schooling proves to be inadequate or inappropriate when they do get one. Their negative feelings result both from the lack of current reinforcement for behaviors that were reinforced previously in school and from punishing consequences.

Another problem (mentioned in Chapter Four) occurs when there is a long delay before school-acquired behavior is reinforced in the outside world. If persons behave in ways learned in school, and if these behaviors are not reinforced, they may extinguish. For example, the well-schooled writer may go for years without finding a market for her or his writings. In the absence of other possible reinforcers, such as attention or admiration from friends, the person is likely to give up writing.

With the much-discussed "crisis in education," Skinner's views have a great deal of current relevance. He believed that young people are a nation's greatest resource and that education should play a stronger part in developing this resource. He indicated what is involved in effective teaching (priming, prompting, and vanishing, with appropriate reinforcement during the process) and suggested a technology for implementing his ideas (teaching machines and programmed instruction). Additionally, he pointed out that educators need to consider carefully the usefulness of what is taught and the likelihood that behaviors acquired in school will be reinforced in the world outside the classroom. A valuable function of Skinner's ideas on education is that they remind us of the basics that all too often are overlooked.

The Quality of Daily Life

Many of Skinner's writings and all of his basic operant-conditioning concepts apply to daily life. In this section, however, the focus will be on the main points of an article published in the May 1986 issue of *American Psychologist,* titled "What Is Wrong with Daily Life in the Western World?" (it is reprinted in Skinner's book *Upon Further Reflection,* 1987a). What follows is my interpretation of what Skinner wrote; others have looked at it somewhat differently (for example, Powell, 1987; Staats, 1988).

Skinner suggested that a major problem of daily life in Western democracies is that the consequences of behaviors frequently have "pleasing effects" at the expense of "strengthening effects." This erodes the contingencies of reinforcement that shape and maintain a wide variety of important behaviors, and feelings of depression, listlessness, and boredom are common. What is at stake is the enjoyment of life: "Where thousands of millions of people in other parts of the world cannot do many of the things they want to do, hundreds of millions in the West do not want to do many of the things they can do" (Skinner, 1986, p. 572).

Isn't there a contradiction here? How can Skinner say that the consequences of our behaviors have pleasing effects and also say that we have lost much of the enjoyment of life? The point is that a consequence may feel good but not necessarily strengthen behavior. For example, good feelings may result from watching TV or going to the movies, hiring someone to do household chores, eating out instead of cooking, driving a luxury car that does almost everything except steer itself, paying others to take care of our children, and so on. In the long run the pleasure may or may not continue to be experienced, but what certainly is lost are the many behaviors that would be strengthened if we were more active ourselves. Our possibilities for enjoying life become more limited when our behaviors become more limited. Consider the extreme case in which a very wealthy person has everything taken care of by others: what is left to enjoy if the pleasing effects of being continually waited on wear off and the person no longer can do things on his or her own? Most of us have not reached this stage, but Skinner warned that we are headed in the direction of losing the strengthening effects that keep our behaviors strong.

He indicated five cultural practices that promote pleasing, rather than strengthening, effects: (1) Workers generally are estranged from the products of their work in modern industries, where jobs are highly specialized. The gain in pleasure derived from the availability of the many goods that are produced efficiently is offset by the loss of work behaviors that are strengthened by immediate consequences, such as those of a craftsperson. (2) We rely on all kinds of help, from labor-saving devices that have made us "button pushers" to social agencies that provide a wide array of services. Some of this is desirable, and it generally feels good when help is obtained, but the situation can result in the loss of valuable behaviors when we are helped too much. (3) Our behavior is increasingly affected by advice; "experts" are everywhere; rule-governed" behavior is on the rise. There is no doubt that advice is essential for acquiring a large repertoire of behavior, and it can be pleasing to receive good advice that saves us time and helps us avoid aversive consequences. However, behavior is likely to be weak when we simply do as we are told and do not experience direct consequences. (4) Many behaviors are influenced by ethical rules and laws, which of course are important to a culture. Pleasure sometimes derives from following them; persons may gain "peace of mind" or a "sense of security." However, the strengthening of behavior through personal consequences often is long delayed when rules and laws are obeyed. (5) The availability of many "pleasures"—exciting spectator sports, entertaining performances, beautiful paintings, delicious foods, and so on—does little to strengthen behaviors that sustain individuals and the culture. What mainly is strengthened by these pleasures is "the behavior that brings one into contact with them" (Skinner, 1986, p. 571).

People in advanced cultures, as suggested by the preceding analysis, suffer from too many opportunities to do things that have pleasing, rather than strengthening, consequences. Skinner believed that weaknesses in behavior that lower the quality of life in the West can be remedied by the field of applied behavior analysis. Contingencies of reinforcement need to be improved so that behavior will be strengthened. Some of this is being done now. For example, in education, therapy, and industry, behavior analysts are helping teachers, therapists, and managers make constructive changes.

Reinforcers need to be contingent on behaviors that are important for the long-term well-being of individuals and the survival of the culture. For example, programmed instruction can be used to strengthen students' behaviors, but it is important that these behaviors be appropriate in the world outside the classroom so that their strength is maintained by "real-world" reinforcers. Persons in therapy also are benefited most if the behaviors that are strengthened with the therapist's help continue to have reinforcing consequences in everyday life. Employees' behaviors can be strengthened by more immediate positive reinforcement, perhaps by seeing how their efforts contribute directly to the final product or service offered. In each of these examples, positive reinforcement maintains the strength of behavior; when this occurs, aversive and punitive measures to get people to behave appropriately are unnecessary. Also, the quality of daily life is enhanced.

Saving the World

In both lectures and writings, Skinner expressed great concern about the future of the world. Environmental pollution, overpopulation, wasteful uses of natural resources, and threats of nuclear war are among the problems that troubled him. He believed that certain behaviors must be changed if these problems are to be alleviated and that a science and technology of behavior is the best means by which this can be accomplished.

The experimental analysis of behavior has shown that the circumstances and consequences of behavior are of vital importance in determining what people do. This finding has strong practical implications: instead of trying to solve major world problems by "changing attitudes" or "appealing to reason," Skinner advised changing the contingencies of reinforcement that cause these problems. For example, overpopulation could be eased by removing social and economic incentives for having children and making effective contraceptive methods easily available. To reduce the pollution and waste of resources that result from millions of people driving their own cars to work, public transportation systems that are faster and safer could be designed; also, other incentives could be added, such as free newspapers, coffee, or snacks for commuters. The development of such systems would be expensive, but there would be future benefits.

The fact that the major benefits lie in the future is the main reason why suggestions about saving the world are frequently ignored. The *immediate* consequences for problem behaviors often are reinforcing. Consider these examples: (1) Industrial pollution occurs partly because of the reinforcing profits from disposing of waste material quickly and easily. (2) There is immediate reinforcement for the sexual behavior that leads to overpopulation. (3) Driving alone to work, and wasting natural resources in the process, is reinforced by ease, comfort, and convenience. (4) Threatening to use nuclear weapons may be reinforced by gaining what is demanded or by stopping the other nation's aversive actions (the latter is a case of negative reinforcement).

Since immediate reinforcement powerfully affects behavior, and possible future outcomes are much less influential, how can the world be saved? Skinner was not sure that it will be. He believed that our governmental, religious, and economic institutions are committed to existing practices; that is, the behaviors of the leaders of these institutions are being reinforced by the consequences that are occurring now, and therefore they are not likely to be affected greatly by warnings about future negative consequences. The main hope lies in a science and technology of behavior that is "free of governmental, religious, and economic ideologies" (Skinner, 1987a, p. 14) and is able to design better cultural practices. These cultural practices could then be maintained and transmitted to new generations through an improved educational system.

The rise of a science and technology of behavior to a dominant position may occur as governmental, religious, and economic institutions become less able to provide the positive reinforcers that result in "security" and "peace of mind." Also, aversive methods (such as threats of punishment) that institutions use to control behavior may become less effective. There already is much talk about the breakdown of society, as many citizens express grave concerns about lawlessness, immorality, and financial mismanagement. With less reinforcement for following traditional rules of behavior espoused by our institutions, reinforcement increasingly may occur for behaviors based on science and technology. Of course, there is no assurance that this will happen. If it doesn't, and if we continue along the present path, Skinner suggested that we and our world may not survive.

Many organizations are concerned about world problems. They attempt to influence institutional leaders by protesting against existing practices and by rallying public support for their protests. What about these organizations? Won't they be able to turn things around? Skinner was skeptical: More than vocal protests are needed to change the contingencies of reinforcement that control the leaders' behaviors. Also, the public tends to avoid or ignore statements and evidence that predict a disastrous fate for the world (these are very aversive stimuli). A more effective approach would be to "offer them a world to which they will turn because of the reinforcing consequences of doing so" (Skinner, 1987a, p. 13). By statements and by example, we should show that positive reinforcers are available for behaviors that do not put us and the world at greater risk.

Managing Old Age

Skinner's interests ranged from the global problem of saving the world to the personal problem of how to cope with old age. He wrote an article titled "Intellectual Self-Management in Old Age" (Skinner, 1983a) and a book, with Margaret E. Vaughan, called *Enjoy Old Age* (Skinner & Vaughan, 1983)—the book has large print, to aid those with failing eyesight. Much of what he wrote was based on his own solutions to the problems of aging.

Skinner apparently dealt well with growing old; he remained active and productive. He continued to lecture occasionally, and to write, until his death. Even in the summer of 1990, when he knew he would die soon of leukemia, he said that he had no anxiety or worry about the end of his life (*New York Times,* August 8, 1990, p. A15). As reported in the November 1990 issue of *American Psychologist* (p. 1203), he worked until the evening before his death on a paper that continued his criticisms of cognitive psychology; the paper was published in that same issue (Skinner, 1990a).

As expected, Skinner coped with the problems of old age by using a behavioristic approach. He emphasized control of one's own behavior and offered many practical hints. For example, (1) to remember the umbrella when rain is predicted, hang it on the doorknob; (2) use short, simple sentences so that digressions are less likely; (3) to remember names of acquaintances at a social function, rehearse their names beforehand; (4) to avoid fatigue, be content with fewer good hours of work per day, and use leisure time for relaxation rather than for complex intellectual activities like chess or difficult puzzles; (5) when old patterns of behavior are not reinforced, behave in different ways—in other words, try something new; (6) to avoid becoming helpless, don't allow others to overdo their helpfulness; (7) to remember important ideas, keep a notepad or recorder handy for use when the ideas occur—"In place of memories, memoranda" (Skinner, 1983a, p. 240).

Contemporary Psychology

Skinner felt strongly that trends in contemporary psychology are blocking the development of a valuable science and technology of behavior. He believed that humanistic psychology, psychotherapy, and cognitive psychology are special threats (Skinner, 1987b). His primary objection to all three was that they emphasize internal determinants of behavior. Behavior itself is seen primarily as the expression of something inside the person; it is explained by referring to concepts such as intelligence, beliefs, imagination, reasoning, actualization, attitudes, expectations, memories, feelings, states of mind, understanding, and mental operations. Behavior is not considered an important subject matter in its own right; therefore the environmental conditions that affect it are not given adequate attention.

Because so many of the concepts used by humanistic psychologists, psychotherapists, and cognitive psychologists are poorly defined, and observable behaviors and environmental conditions are not given sufficient attention, a useful science and technology based on these fields is unlikely. In contrast, Skinner believed, a science and technology based on the experimental analysis of behavior can be effective. This approach supports the solving of behavioral problems by changing the contingencies of reinforcement, rather than by changing expectations, attitudes, feelings, states of mind, or some other supposed internal determinants of behavior. Very unfortunately, according to Skinner, contemporary trends in psychology are not favorable for the expansion of such an approach, and the search for internal causes goes on.

In an article titled "Cognitive Science and Behaviorism," Skinner (1987a, p. 111) made specific accusations against cognitive scientists, further clarifying his objections to current psychological trends. Briefly, he criticized them for (1) considering the brain as a storage space, (2) having no appropriate method for observing internal processes, (3) accepting subjects' verbal reports as scientific data, (4) accepting feelings and states of mind as causes of behavior, (5) making claims that the "depths of human behavior" are being explored, and (6) engaging in speculation without adequate definitions or logical thinking.

The first criticism perhaps needs more explanation. It is based on Skinner's straightforward assumptions that (1) behavior is changed by certain events, such as reinforcement or punishment, and (2) neurologists and physiologists eventually will be able to describe the neurophysiological changes that accompany these changes in behavior. The "neurophysiological changes" do *not* involve the storage of information in the brain; the information-processing model that has been popular among some psychologists is alien to Skinner's approach.

In Skinner's view, we don't store and process information as a prelude to further behavior. Rather, we respond behaviorally *and* neurophysiologically in certain ways as a result of environmental conditions. He drew an analogy between a hot filament that emits light, and a person who emits behavior (Skinner, 1987a, p. 101). Just as there is no light *in* the filament, there is no behavior *in* the person; light is not stored in the filament, nor is behavior stored in the person. Instead, when certain conditions exist, the filament changes and emits light, and the person changes and emits behavior.

Again and again in his writings, Skinner warned of the pitfalls of conceiving of behavior as emerging from within. In the last paper on which he worked (Skinner, 1990a), he repeated this theme, suggesting strongly that psychologists stop trying to build a science based on an "initiating self" or a "creative mind." He advised turning to the study of how behaviors are selected by the environment; one way of studying this is by operant-conditioning procedures.

Media Advice

Skinner's views on misguided searches for inner causes of behavior apply to many areas of society. For example, newspapers and popular magazines often suggest that personal and social problems result from inner weaknesses. Also, the solutions offered frequently rely on fixing something internal. In this section, I use

Skinner's ideas as a basis for evaluating these tendencies and their consequences and for making recommendations. Further extensions of his concepts are contained in Chapter Eight.

Consider the italicized words in the following statements:

"The answer to positive life changes is inside each of us. We must tap that *inner potential.*"

"Once you get in touch with your *basic feelings* and *emotions,* you can become a better functioning, more fulfilled person."

"With the proper *state of mind* and enough *willpower,* many problems can be overcome."

"*Drive* and *initiative* are necessary for success."

"Adversity can be conquered by the indomitable human *spirit.*"

"If today's generation had more *moral fiber,* our current social problems could be solved."

"Employees' *attitudes* about work have to be changed if the United States is going to be known once again as a producer of quality products."

"Political *courage* and *conviction* are needed if we are to stand up to foreign threats to our nation."

"If our society is to survive, the *character* of our young people must be strengthened."

These types of statements are common. They can be read every day. Often they are made by authoritative writers. What they share is the attempt to explain or give advice about personal and social problems by focusing inward, toward inner potential, feelings, emotions, states of mind, willpower, drive, initiative, spirit, moral fiber, attitudes, courage, conviction, character, and so on. There is an overwhelming array of internal states that are referred to as causes or cures of various problems.

A problem exists in differentiating these states from one another. For example, what are the differences among willpower, drive, and initiative, or between moral fiber and character? Despite the obvious difficulties of determining exactly what these terms mean and how they differ, they continue to be used, with full confidence that something important is being said.

The tendency to focus inward has disadvantages beyond the vagueness of the terms used. Most important, it distracts us from more concrete, practical, and potentially beneficial approaches. We get sidetracked from analyzing and changing the outward sources of our problems.

Inner explanations occur in many different contexts, and examples can be collected easily. Here are just a few recent instances:

A newspaper article on how to raise children states that the effective parent is one who is *fulfilled and feels good about himself or herself.*

An article on our educational system suggests that teachers need more *spirit* if they are going to do a better job.

A columnist suggests that violence results from inadequate control over the *dark impulses within us.*

A criminal-justice professor says that people commit crimes because of *feelings of alienation and despair*.

A newsmagazine asks if the United States has the *will* to deal with the garbage crisis before it becomes intolerable.

A reporter says that lack of *will and self-respect* in this country is the cause of our deteriorating highways and bridges.

In some of these examples, possible external explanations or solutions were not ignored completely: effective parenting was seen as requiring specific medical, nutritional, and child-development training; in the education article, it was pointed out that teachers need more status and fewer bureaucratic demands; the criminal-justice professor said that deprived environments contribute to crime; the article on coping with the garbage crisis suggested specific steps that would help alleviate the situation; the news-service reporter made the point that there is little recognition or praise for politicians who push for funds for highway and bridge repairs.

In every one of these cases, however, external factors ultimately were subordinated to internal factors. Instead of persistently focusing on the real-world conditions that affect parenting, education, crime, and even garbage disposal and highway and bridge maintenance, improvements in these areas were seen, in the last analysis, as dependent on some internal change or on the motivating influence of some internal force. The message seems to be: "Yes, there are various things we can do about our problems, but what's really needed is an infusion of spirit or willpower, or a different attitude or frame of mind, among those involved." But how will this come about? Here we usually are left up in the air.

We also are sometimes "left up in the air" by psychologists. For example, a psychologist writes clearly and concisely about various remedies for human aggression. He suggests, among other things, that children be taught nonaggressive behaviors, that we stop reinforcing tough, macho-type behaviors, and that we try to reduce frustrating, aversive situations that help produce aggressive responses. So far, so good. But he doesn't follow through with concrete, practical advice about how to implement these suggestions. Admittedly, this would be very difficult to do, but we are not helped at all when he says that we seem to lack "the will and conviction" to bring about the needed changes. If such inner states are necessary for external changes to take place, we are in a real bind. What will cause these states to occur?

One answer to this dilemma emerges if we take a perspective derived from Skinner's views: if people faced with an important problem have an appropriate repertoire of behavior (in common language, if they know *what* to do and *how* to do it), they are more likely to take action. The motivation to act does not have to come from within; rather, the troublesome situation often provides its own motivation. In Skinner's terms, aversive stimuli often result in behaviors that will reduce the stimuli; in more familiar terms, if we are bothered by something, we usually want to change it. However, what to do and how to do it are often unclear.

Generally, when there seems to be a *lack of initiative,* what actually is lacking is the means to act; this is more likely to come from without (a result of one's history of reinforcement) than from within. Behaviors that commonly are said to reflect *will, conviction, spirit, drive,* and so on result from an appropriate behavioral repertoire; inner states referred to as *confidence,* a *good attitude,* and the *right frame of mind* are other results. If success or acknowledgment comes from one's actions, feelings of *pride* and *self-respect* are likely to occur.

The point is this: many of the inner qualities that we refer to are actually products of external conditions and behaviors. From a Skinnerian perspective, these qualities do not occur spontaneously or independently. Therefore, rather than simply assuming that some people have good qualities and others don't, or wishing that these qualities would increase, we would be better off trying to change conditions and behaviors (that is, contingencies of reinforcement) so that more people (including ourselves) would have the desirable characteristics that we admire.

Following this line of reasoning, those who write about individual or social problems would serve us best if they helped to detail specifically what conditions and behaviors are troublesome and what can be done to change them. We are not served well by statements about the necessity of spirit, willpower, commitment, self-respect, moral fiber, courage, or other inner qualities. It's often a very tough job to find the critical conditions and behaviors that need changing, and it may be even harder to bring about the necessary changes. Not all of our personal and social problems can be solved, but focusing on inner causes diverts us from the things that *can* be done.

Sometimes the extent to which inner causes dominate our thinking is dramatic. I'll close this section with two brief examples that illustrate vividly how external conditions may be subordinated to inner explanations. These are not isolated examples; if one pays attention, similar instances can be found quite frequently in the media.

An article in a well-known newsmagazine (*Time,* December 3, 1979, pp. 55–56) told of the horrible conditions that Cambodian refugees had been exposed to by the regime of Premier Pol Pot. Reportedly they had experienced the murders of parents and children and undergone brutal physical punishments, were constantly under surveillance by informants, and were dealt with severely if they expressed sorrow over their losses. The result was certain bizarre behaviors by the refugees; for example, some of them would laugh when seeing someone in pain. Despite the seemingly obvious explanation of such behavior as being due to exposure to extremely harsh external conditions, the doctors who treated the refugees' physical ailments were puzzled by their behavior and wondered if *something in their personalities* made them act so strangely.

An equal fascination with inner states and insufficient attention to the powerful effects of external circumstances can be found in a review of *The Ik,* a play based on Colin Turnbull's book *The Mountain People* (*Newsweek,* October 25, 1976, pp. 99, 101). The Ik, tribal hunters in northern Uganda, were deprived of their hunting grounds by the government, and they began to starve. The situation became dire; their society began to disintegrate. Apathetic behavior punctuated by cruelty became common as conditions worsened. The reviewer's conclusion about these behaviors did not focus primarily on the effects of being without food but rather on what he assumed to be an *inner failing of the will* of these people.

Skinner's concepts and perspectives apply in many ways to today's world. *Walden Two* and *Beyond Freedom and Dignity* were direct attempts on his part to extend his basic views to broad social issues. Also, Skinner believed that (1) education would be greatly improved by more attention to priming, prompting, and vanishing, which can be accomplished through the use of programmed instruction; (2) the quality of daily life could be improved if appropriate behaviors were strengthened by positive reinforcement; (3) the saving of the world from its problems was most likely to occur through a science and technology of behavior; (4) managing old age could be accomplished best by relying on behavioral procedures; and (5) contemporary psychology was focused too much on the search for inner causes of behavior. Additionally, his ideas can be applied to modern media advice, which often subordinates external influences to internal influences when personal and social problems are being evaluated.

EIGHT

Author's Reflections and Concluding Comments

IN THIS CHAPTER I discuss Skinnerian psychology in more personal terms, indicating what I believe to be some of the most important influences that it can have in our everyday lives. More of my own views and examples are presented than in previous chapters. Actually, of course, this whole book reflects my perspectives on Skinner. Throughout, I've selected and emphasized certain portions of his writings, using examples and making interpretations that I believe clarify his work. While doing this, I've tried to convey his ideas without altering their essential content. In this chapter I continue in that general vein but with a bit more extrapolation.

Being positively affected by Skinner's concepts can occur very dramatically (that is, a person can become a thoroughgoing radical behaviorist), or it can result in varying degrees of acceptance. On the other hand, some persons seem to reject *everything* he said simply because they disagree with certain aspects of his approach; this is unfortunate. His suggestions cover a wide variety of important issues and ways of looking at the behaviors of ourselves and others, and they can be useful even when they aren't accepted totally. In other words, there's no need to discard the whole approach even if parts of it are found objectionable.

As I indicated in the Preface, I find much of what Skinner said to be very reasonable and useful, although I'm not sure that all the answers to life's situations and problems are to be found in radical behaviorism. I continue trying to apply it and to test out its assumptions in everyday life. For me it has proved to be a very satisfactory way of interpreting much of what goes on in my own life, in the lives of others, and in society at large. Perhaps I should point out that I don't walk around all day thinking "What would Skinner say about this?" or "What would Skinner do in this situation?" Rather, I simply try to think in behavioristic terms when some behavior—my own or someone else's—or some situation needs interpreting. Also, I try to apply some behavioristic concepts to improve my behavior.

Self-Help

In this section I'll comment briefly on some aspects of "self-help"; other relevant material is discussed in later sections. Most of us are concerned at times with improving the ways we feel and behave. "Self-help" is one of the areas in which we often turn inward instead of trying persistently to understand and change the external conditions at work, at home, in our social lives, and so forth that frequently are the real causes of our problems. We get loads of advice from radio and television counselors, popular books, and magazine articles to the effect that we can live fuller, more satisfying lives if we get to know our true, innermost selves and get rid of negative, counterproductive feelings such as guilt and inferiority. The answers, in other words, are somewhere inside us. Unfortunately, much of this advice is based simply on the adviser's faith that "looking within" will help. There is a lack of solid evidence to support most self-help approaches, but that doesn't stop the onslaught of "discover-your-inner-self" advice.

Perhaps part of the appeal of such advice is that we don't have to change, at least not immediately, the status quo of our everyday lives. We can work on problems within rather than doing something specific about troublesome ongoing behaviors or circumstances. However, it is very likely that the status quo does need to be changed; turning inward for answers can simply be a way of turning away from the tough task of changing behaviors and conditions that are causing problems (in other words, "turning inward" may be negatively reinforced).

The details of living—for example, the jobs we have and the ways we do these jobs, our relationships and the ways these relationships are carried on, the ways we spend our spare time, and various personal habits such as what we eat, how much we sleep, and how much exercise we get—need to be looked at carefully to see what effects they are having. When the effects are negative or not as good as we would like, alterations are in order.

Instead of following some self-discovery path, we might derive more benefits by taking a cue from Skinner and applying a procedure from an unlikely source: experimental methodology. Put simply, the idea is to change something and see what happens. Sooner or later, if one's life is to be improved, real changes in the real world have to be made. It would seem preferable to do this sooner rather than later, and too much concentration on our inner states may cause unnecessary and damaging delays.

Sometimes even a minor, seemingly insignificant, external change, such as the order in which job responsibilities are handled, the tone of voice used when talking to one's spouse or children, or the scheduling of meals and what is eaten at each meal, might have more dramatic effects than would a good deal of introspective probing. It's largely a matter of experimentation: changing everyday details to see if the effects are desirable. Most of us can do this to greater or lesser extents.

This experimental approach to self-improvement may sound simple and superficial compared with self-help approaches that dwell on feelings and emotions (probably because we're so used to thinking that change *must* involve looking within our personalities). Actually, it isn't an easy approach. It's often very difficult to figure out exactly what behaviors or external conditions need to be changed, how to change them, and how to observe the effects accurately. This is where self-help advisers might best apply themselves—helping people to accomplish these often difficult tasks.

An important point is that, when a "good" change in external behaviors or conditions is made, it eventually results in improved feelings and states of mind. This is the opposite process from that implied in much self-help advice. Commonly we hear and read that, if we get our feelings and thoughts straightened out, we'll be able to behave more constructively and productively. It's more likely the other way around: if we get our behaviors and circumstances straightened out, then we'll feel and think better.

Positive Reinforcement in Interpersonal Relations

A fundamental concept of Skinnerian psychology is positive reinforcement: behaviors are strengthened if they are followed by certain stimuli (which are called positive reinforcers). Many of the important positive reinforcers in everyday life—attention, approval, appreciation, and affection—are given and received through social interactions. Not only does positive reinforcement strengthen behavior, but often it causes the recipient to have "good feelings." These facts have been pointed out repeatedly in previous chapters, but we should look at positive reinforcement one more time. It's a prime example of a Skinnerian concept that can have great value in one's life (even if certain other aspects of Skinner's approach aren't accepted).

Positive reinforcement seems very simple. In fact, it seems so simple that often it is overlooked. We frequently don't provide reinforcement when we should. Many times we "expect" individuals to behave well and therefore fail to reinforce their good behaviors positively when they occur. This is true in teacher/student, parent/child, supervisor/worker, wife/husband, friend/friend, and other types of relationships. We don't notice or we overlook good behavior, as though somehow it is supposed to occur without any external influence. This goes back to the traditional idea that people should behave well because of inner motivations; that is, they should "want" to be good, they should have the "desire" to behave well, and they should have enough "common sense" to know what the correct behaviors are. I still find myself falling into this type of thinking occasionally, but it's nonproductive. As much as we may wish that others would "instinctively" be nice, considerate, and so forth, their behaviors are influenced by their past and present circumstances. If those circumstances don't include positive reinforcement for desirable behaviors, such behaviors are unlikely to occur.

An interesting aspect of human interactions is that we often are more likely to show appreciation when strangers or casual acquaintances are courteous or helpful than we are when those close to us behave in these ways. We tend to grow lax in acknowledging the positive actions of those whom we know well. This eventually can lead to poor relationships with few mutually reinforcing interactions. *Intermittent reinforcement* (for details, see Chapter Two) generally maintains the considerate and loving behaviors involved in intimate relationships; in other words, sometimes these behaviors are acknowledged and appreciation is shown, and sometimes they aren't. This is fine to a certain extent, but serious problems arise when *many* such behaviors are ignored, causing them to occur very infrequently or to stop completely (technically, *extinction* occurs). When this happens, the relationship is in bad shape.

Skinner's writings are helpful here. They can change our behaviors and make our relationships more satisfying because they point out the importance of positive reinforcement. Since studying Skinnerian psychology, I find myself more likely to regularly express appreciation for the things those close to me do to make my life more comfortable and enjoyable (however, not being perfect, I still let too many opportunities to reinforce these behaviors slip by). Expressing appreciation (and this doesn't mean "wearing it out" by saying "thank you" or by going into dramatic gestures for every little thing) has two important outcomes: (1) it makes it more likely that nice things will continue to be done for me (thereby making me feel good), and (2) it makes the persons doing them feel good. Of course, I too am susceptible to positive reinforcement, so my behaviors also are affected by the appreciation I receive from others. In short, reinforcement works in both directions. I believe that Skinner was right when he said that our behaviors are strongly determined by our environmental conditions, and the best conditions are those in which positive reinforcement prevails.

It's easy to believe that intimate relationships transcend mundane considerations such as positive reinforcement, but these relationships can be interpreted in large part by using this concept. "Love" frequently is discussed in almost mystical terms in our society, but the fact that new lovers often heap positive reinforcers (compliments, attention, affection, gifts, sex, and so on) on each other is most likely responsible for their feelings of being "deeply in love." It's a case of mutual positive reinforcement.*

The deterioration of intense relationships sometimes may be the result of *too much* initial reinforcement. It's next to impossible in the long run for two people to be the sole sources of positive reinforcement for each other. Though romances may begin in that vein, other reinforcers eventually beckon again, such as those found in performing one's work, seeing friends, playing sports, or pursuing hobbies. If this occurs unevenly (one person turns more to outside reinforcers than the other), problems seem especially likely to arise; disruption of intense mutual reinforcement can be very disturbing, particularly if other sources of positive reinforcement are not readily available. The neglected partner

---

*Negative reinforcement also can play a role in intensifying and maintaining relationships. If doing things with a certain person removes aversive stimuli associated with situations such as working at a monotonous job, being all alone, or being with other people who are critical, the behaviors that produce contact with that person are strengthened. Negative reinforcement can have effects within relationships as well. To give just one example, when arguing is followed closely by sexual activity, sex may be both negatively reinforced (it removes the aversive stimuli of arguing) and positively reinforced (it produces an orgasm).

may start complaining or making threats (thereby introducing aversive stimuli), causing the other to avoid the relationship (which will be negatively reinforcing—see Chapter Two) and perhaps find more and more reinforcement elsewhere. And so it goes, until the relationship breaks up or is characterized by bickering and arguing (or, because both breaking up and arguing can be very aversive, the couple may stay together but spend their time with each other in silence or in talking about trivial, noncontroversial subjects).

Skinner's concepts are relevant to these situations. Initially, it seems to me, it's important to realize that positive reinforcers are found in many different types of situations and activities, and not to behave as though one situation or one person will supply *everything*. Such behaviors too often lead to failure (perhaps accounting partly for the high divorce rate that exists), with accompanying feelings of disappointment, guilt, resentment, anger, and so on (remember, Skinner agreed that unpleasant feelings can arise from certain environmental events, and certainly the deterioration of a relationship would classify as such an event).

What I have just suggested in no way rules out feelings of love. When we interact in certain intimate and reinforcing ways, we feel reactions that we have learned to label as "love." This doesn't need to be continually analyzed in detail or spoiled by cold objectivity. In other words, it's fine to relax and enjoy "being in love," but it seems wise to try to maintain a good thing, and positive reinforcement plays an important role.

As indicated, behaving as though the *only* positive reinforcements in life will come from one's lover is almost certain to lead to problems, very likely in the form of one or both partners eventually using aversive methods of control to try to maintain the continual flow of positive reinforcers. On the other hand, lovers who regularly behave in positively reinforcing ways toward each other *but avoid being each other's only source of reinforcement* are apt to experience more enduring satisfactions. With some consistency, we should be sure to reinforce those behaviors that are important in our relationships. If we don't, they may gradually disappear (extinguish). Then we will be left wondering "What happened between us? It used to be so great, and now it's gone." It's easy to think that good, lasting relationships happen "naturally," but partners who continue to recognize and appreciate (reinforce) each other's considerate and loving behaviors (and avoid trying to control each other's behavior by threats or punishments) are tipping the scales heavily in their favor. Recently, in a newspaper article, a man happily married for 43 years said that simple, thoughtful little things maintain his and his wife's love. This seems to me to be another way of saying that positive reinforcers are important.

Intimate relationships, of course, are not the only interpersonal situations to which positive reinforcement applies. It is relevant whenever persons interact. As Skinner made clear, there's a lot of aversive control in the world and too little appropriate use of positive reinforcement. Threats, subtle or direct, are used frequently to get people to do what is expected of them. In the following example, desirable behaviors consistently were ignored until they eventually dropped to near zero in occurrence, whereupon threats were used to try to restore the behaviors.

Many years ago I worked in a factory alongside a new employee who was fairly effective at his job. The supervisor, for some reason unknown to me, never acknowledged this man's work. In fact, he generally ignored him completely. Gradually the man's performance level decreased to a pathetic level (in technical terms, it *extinguished*). At this point, the supervisor started harassing him and threatened to have him transferred to a less desirable department (the use of *aversive control*). The worker then stepped up his production (which was *negatively reinforced*— that is, this behavior was strengthened because it removed the aversive stimuli of harassment and threats). As is common with aversive control, however, it not only had the immediate desirable effect of increasing the worker's output, but it also had some undesirable effects: he had difficulties learning new tasks, he complained bitterly to his co-workers about the supervisor and the job, he started having physical ailments, and eventually he quit the job.

This man proved during his first few weeks at work that he could do an effective job. However, the total absence of positive feedback about his performance (lack of reinforcing comments from the supervisor) gradually led to a situation involving aversive control, and this paved the way to his leaving the job in order to escape the aversive conditions. I've often thought about this case. A little positive reinforcement would have gone a long way. I also believe that it is a common example. Workers, as well as persons in other kinds of situations, often do not get sufficient positive feedback about their good performance and therefore don't function nearly as effectively as they could. However, before putting blame on supervisors or others who are in charge, remember that they too are affected by their circumstances. The whole system may need to be evaluated in order to see why aversive control is used so often.

Before leaving the topic of positive reinforcement in interpersonal relations, a few words of caution are in order. It isn't sufficient simply to supply more reinforcers to those with whom we interact. They must be applied to behaviors in a discriminating way if they are to have beneficial results. Positive reinforcers strengthen the behaviors they follow, so we should be sure that a behavior is desirable before we reinforce it. Parents who give in to the temper tantrums of their children, employees who yield to unfair requests from their employers, wives or husbands who give up valued activities because of spouses' complaints, teachers who approve the inadequate work of their students, and individuals who go along with the inconsiderate demands of their friends—all are examples of persons who are positively reinforcing undesirable behaviors. We need more positive reinforcement in the world, but it should be applied discriminately. Inappropriate positive reinforcement does more harm than good.

When it is appropriate to use positive reinforcement, it is essential to find something that will work as a positive reinforcer. Occasionally, attempts to reinforce good behavior with attention, affection, praise, gifts, and so on do not work. Although in many cases these are effective reinforcers, sometimes they fail to strengthen desired behavior. When this happens, they cannot be considered reinforcers, and the search for something more effective must continue. What is actually a reinforcer may depend on the particular person, behavior, and/or occasion.

Assigning Blame

Being influenced by Skinner's writings is likely to change, at least to some extent, the tendency to blame others for their behaviors, however annoying or harmful they may be. When we blame others, we censure them and hold them responsible for their actions. In everyday life it's difficult not to do this. This practice is part of our cultural tradition, and most of us have learned it well. Sometimes it's effective in curtailing undesirable behaviors, at least temporarily. To avoid further blame, persons may avoid repeating condemned behaviors. Also, the *threat* of blame sometimes gets people to behave "properly." The basic message is: "If you don't do as expected, you will be considered irresponsible and held to blame."

Despite the fact that punitive or aversive methods of control (such as assigning blame) are sometimes effective, they have serious drawbacks. As discussed before, their outcomes are unpredictable. Will the person do as requested, or will she or he leave the situation? Will the person avoid the situation in the future? Will the person counterattack? Will the person complain bitterly or behave in other disturbing ways? Even if the person does as requested in the presence of the controller, will he or she continue to do so when the controller isn't around? Besides raising these questions, punishment and aversive control produce undesirable emotional responses in those on whom they are used. Persons certainly are not happy or satisfied when they are being controlled by such methods.

The point is this: even if it's assumed that individuals are responsible for their behaviors, and therefore assigning blame for objectionable actions is justified, it doesn't consistently work well and it causes ill feelings. There is ample evidence for the long-range failure of this approach. Despite our extensive history of blaming people for all sorts of undesirable activities, these activities are still common.

In Skinner's approach, assigning blame is inappropriate, because there is no personal responsibility in the traditional sense. When someone does something annoying or harmful, the question is "What's wrong with the person's environment or environmental history?" and not "What's wrong with him (her)?" This way of looking at things requires a major shift from our usual viewpoint. Also, it sometimes can be a very burdensome approach, because the critical environmental conditions may be hard to find and may be difficult, or even impossible, to change. Being a radical behaviorist often requires great persistence. It's often much quicker and simpler to say "It's your fault. You're to blame." Of course, when critical environmental conditions can't be found and controlled in order to change offensive behaviors, then it is very likely that punitive or aversive methods such as assigning blame will be used.

My own efforts to find environmental causes of behaviors have been reinforced sufficiently to keep me going in that direction, although I sometimes catch myself blaming others for certain actions (especially when other responses are not reinforced). Blame basically is useless, except perhaps as a temporary measure when more effective methods are unavailable. If the environmental conditions causing the offensive behaviors (conditions such as reinforcement for offensive behaviors or lack of opportunities and reinforcement for more desirable behaviors) can be found and changed, the behaviors that are of concern will change. If these environmental conditions can't be altered, then blame still is unlikely to do an adequate job. It may even aggravate the problem. This is especially true when alternative, desirable behaviors are unlikely to be emitted by the offending individual, so that there are no improved behaviors to reinforce positively. Still, it must be remembered that blaming is a likely response when other methods of control can't be applied effectively.

How can more people be convinced of the inefficiency of assigning blame and encouraged to seek out and change environmental conditions? One way is by reading Skinner's writings or other behavioristic information, such as that contained in this book. They may then apply the approach in their own lives (rule-governed behavior). If the approach is effective (reinforced), it will then continue to be used (the use of the approach will become contingency-shaped rather than rule-governed).

Important practical questions arise if it's assumed that personal responsibility and blame are not applicable to human behavior: "What should be done with persons who are dangerous to others or who carry out criminal activities? Should such persons be allowed to run around free until we find the environmental causes of their behaviors and change those causes?" Though arguments *for* environmental determinism, and *against* personal responsibility and blame, might seem to imply an excessively lenient approach to dangerous or criminal actions, such is not necessarily the case. For practical reasons of public safety and well-being, persons who behave in these ways may have to be institutionalized or imprisoned, but *not* for revenge or to make them "pay for their crimes."

At the present, despite the fact that I believe the environment is the key to both "right" and "wrong" behaviors (with the possible exception of persons who act in disruptive or criminal ways because of brain damage or other neurophysiological abnormalities), I realize that we don't know all of the critical environmental determinants or how to change them. Skinner put us on the right track, but much work remains. In the meantime, until we can construct a society in which harmful behaviors are much less prevalent, and until we know with certainty how to change such behaviors when they occur, it will be necessary to provide the safeguard of confining certain individuals. The essential point, however, is that we should *not* behave as though confinement is giving the person "what he or she deserves." It should be considered a practical step to protect the public.

There is a big difference between confinement as punishment and confinement as a practical matter (though admittedly, to the institutionalized or imprisoned person, the difference might not be clear). In the former case, we continue to hold individuals personally responsible for their actions and to blame them when they fail to act appropriately. This approach has been used for a very long time with highly questionable results. In the latter case, we continue to seek out the environmental causes of behavior, to change these conditions to promote better behaviors, and to develop methods for modifying undesirable or harmful behaviors when they occur. This type of approach has been used with considerable success during recent years by behaviorists working in many different types of settings (clinical, school, family, institutional, and so on) to modify a wide variety of behaviors. If we follow Skinner's advice, we'll work toward much broader and more effective applications. Assigning blame and holding individuals personally responsible for what they do can inhibit progress in this direction. To the extent that our time and efforts are taken up with blaming, accusing, censuring, and so on, we will have less time and energy to examine the environmental determinants of behavior.

Self-Blame and "Turning Inward"

Along with our strong cultural tradition of blaming *others,* we sometimes blame *ourselves* for "improper behaviors" or "signs of weakness." Here is another area in which I've been influenced by Skinner, who wrote: "I have learned to accept my mistakes by referring them to a personal history which was not of my making and could not be changed" (Skinner, 1983c, p. 30). Though I still accuse myself at times of being stupid, irrational, inconsistent, and so on, I do relatively little of this self-condemnation compared to times past.

I've found that blaming myself gets me nowhere. It may have the reinforcing effect of reducing the condemnation of others (if we blame ourselves, others sometimes are less likely to add their blame to the situation), but it doesn't change the basic environmental causes of stupid, irrational, or inconsistent behaviors. I, as well as others, do these things because of circumstances such as inadequate learning (which causes us to behave "stupidly"), the presence of aversive conditions (which we escape or avoid, often in "irrational" ways), and conflicting consequences of our behaviors (if a particular behavior has been both reinforced and punished, we are apt to behave "inconsistently"). These are the types of causes that I now tend to look for when my own behaviors disturb me.

Focusing on "What's wrong with the environment and how can it be changed?" rather than "What's wrong with me?" can often have beneficial and long-lasting effects. However, there are potential problems. As indicated before, critical environmental conditions (such as subtle aversive stimuli or lack of appropriate reinforcements) may be difficult to identify and, once identified, difficult to change. Obvious environmental conditions aren't necessarily changed easily either. For example, a woman who stops blaming herself for being depressed and starts looking for external reasons might quickly find causes in a boring job, an irritable or sarcastic employer, or an extremely jealous husband. Changing such causes, however clear they may be, can be a tough process.

Given these problems, a person attempting to take a behavioristic approach to life may "give up" (extinguish) before she or he has had the chance to see its effectiveness (that is, before reinforcement occurs). In order to prevent the extinction of attempts to locate and change important environmental conditions, it's essential to receive some reinforcement for these efforts. Therefore, if you decide to give the Skinnerian approach a try, don't tackle the biggest and perhaps most difficult situations first. There usually are minor changes that can be made at the start, at least some of which are likely to be effective (reinforcing). These positive consequences help ensure that the approach will be continued.

The depressed woman just mentioned should perhaps begin by making minor changes. Maybe she could change something about the way she does her job (for example, altering the sequence of tasks) or the physical setting in which she works (perhaps rearranging the furniture or doing some minor decorating). Self-monitoring might help: keeping track of work output sometimes is reinforcing in itself and sometimes can help things go more smoothly. A chart showing work progress provides visible evidence that something is being accomplished and also can indicate the times during the workday when efficiency usually drops off (these may be times when breaks should be scheduled). She could try to do something enjoyable during her lunch hour (reading, shopping, eating with a friend, and so on). Some different ways of relating to her employer or husband could be attempted (perhaps a bit more assertiveness, or a bit less, depending on the circumstances). Also, she might ask them to make some small changes (for example, to give her more opportunity to try things on her own before they give advice.)

These particular suggestions might not work for everyone; actual change programs need to be tailored to the individual case. I am simply trying to indicate that there are constructive alternatives to self-blame (or blaming others) when one has problems. By proceeding as suggested, the woman probably would do at least some things that would have positive effects. She then would be likely to continue making changes, and her mood would also be likely to change for the better. At some point a relatively dramatic change, such as quitting her job, confronting her employer, or divorcing her husband, might occur. On the other hand, less drastic changes might be sufficiently reinforcing, and her depression alleviated, so that more extreme actions would never occur.

Of course, our hypothetical woman could continue to blame herself for her depressed condition and turn inward, focusing intensely on her depressed feelings, examining in detail her "inner self," and ruminating about her "personality flaws." The unfortunate aspect of this, besides the continued unpleasant emotions that she would experience, is that it would detract from the direct alteration of her circumstances and behaviors. A basic question is: "Excluding certain changes induced by drugs, illnesses, and other such chemical or physiological conditions, are our feelings or states of mind (depression, anxiety, low self-esteem, and so on) likely to change unless environmental and behavioral changes occur?"

I agree with Skinner's suggestion that they are not. A behavioristic approach begins where other approaches indirectly end up in the long run: with behaviors and the conditions that control them. Evaluating and altering situations, behaviors, and behavioral consequences (that is, contingencies of reinforcement), rather than relying on introspection, are essential for overcoming dreary personal situations. Skinner suggested that we're wasting our time when we don't go directly to the modification of our behaviors through environmental control.

We often believe that we "got over a bad mood" or "straightened out our thinking" because we turned inward and engaged in self-examination. Though that may *seem* to be the case, it's quite possible that while we were introspecting, external behavioral and environmental changes occurred, affecting our emotions and thoughts. For example, an athlete who performs poorly during an important sporting event may develop strong feelings of inadequacy and inferiority. A year later he may be performing at a higher level than ever before. When asked about this, he might say: "I did a lot of thinking and self-examination during this past year. I thought about my motives and my bad feelings. I feel I've found some answers inside myself. I'm not putting myself down anymore, and I've got the will to win. I'm doing pretty well now."

We're accustomed to hearing these kinds of explanations (not only from athletes but from people in general), and we tend to accept them as the real explanations for improved behaviors and feelings. A behavioristic analysis, however, might reveal other factors. To use the example of the athlete, during the past year he may have changed his diet and training techniques based on advice from others (rule-governed behavior), thereby upgrading his performance. Then he may have entered and won several competitions, resulting in consistent improvements in ability and state of mind. Also, he may have had a coach, close friends, relatives, and others who encouraged and praised his efforts. Luckily for him, these conditions prevailed at the same time that he was "focusing inward" and "self-examining"; if he had engaged only in introspective behaviors, it's unlikely that he would have finished the year in winning form.

In short, it is likely that changed circumstances and behaviors account for this athlete's high performance level *and* for his good feelings about himself. As he sees it, and as many people would believe, he analyzed his inner states, they changed, and therefore his performance improved. The difference between this explanation and a behavioristic one is that the former emphasizes the changing of feelings, which then causes behavioral changes. The latter suggests that changed environmental conditions (such as a different diet and training program, a series of successes, and the support of those close to him) caused his improved performance and better emotional condition.

But, it might be asked, "Didn't he make up his mind to change his diet and his training procedures? Wasn't that an act of will?" Perhaps, but not according to a behavioristic analysis, which suggests that environmental events (such as a losing performance) resulted in behaviors (changing his diet and training methods) that would change the aversive condition of "losing." Simply put, the events that occurred in the athlete's life, not some "choice" or "decision," determined his behaviors. "Why did he come back to win, whereas others might have given up?" The answer to this question, from a behavioristic perspective, would involve a detailed look at the circumstances surrounding each individual case. Maybe the athlete who "gives up" doesn't have the support of intimate friends, doesn't discover improved techniques, or has several critical defeats in a row because of stiff competition. Also, events earlier in a person's life can be key factors.

As much as we would like to believe that positive changes in behavior are due to "making up our minds" or "showing willpower," I think that Skinner's suggestions are vital: Environmental circumstances significantly affect our behaviors, and we ought to focus on beneficially altering these circumstances. Self-blame and accompanying introspective analyses will likely distract us from going directly to the environmental influences on our behaviors.

Each person has to look at his or her own environment and behaviors in order to know what to modify. For example, smokers and overeaters (some of whom do a lot of self-blaming for their indulgences) might be able to reduce consumption by avoiding certain situations in which those behaviors are especially likely to occur, and they may cut down even further by doing things that are incompatible with smoking or overeating (such as exercising or playing sports). Another aid is to set up the situation so that some reinforcement (taking a short trip, buying something special, going to a movie) is dependent on staying away from cigarettes or fattening foods for a specified length of time. All of these methods involve changes in environmental conditions.

For heavy smokers or those with serious weight problems, such methods may need to be supplemented by professional help in planning and carrying out behavior-modification programs. In any case, the emphasis should shift from self-blame to constructive alterations of environmental conditions (that is, staying away from situations in which "temptations" are especially likely, putting oneself in circumstances in which incompatible behaviors are required, setting things up so that more desirable behaviors get reinforced, and so on).

Self-blame is far less likely to have positive results than are these types of measures. A behavioristic motto could be "Stop blaming yourself and start changing your environment." Remember, though: if a behavior-modification program is to continue being used, using it *must* be reinforced. Small changes that are likely to have at least a minor positive effect can maintain the approach as you move toward the solution of larger problems (see the references at the beginning of Chapter Seven for more information on behavior modification).

To finish off the topics of self-blame and the inefficiency of focusing inward to find answers to our problems, let's look again at the situation mentioned earlier in this chapter: the deterioration of an intimate relationship. When things start going wrong, typically there are self-doubts and feelings of anxiety, guilt, depression, and so on. Self-accusations are common, with one or both individuals thinking: "What's wrong with me? Is it my fault? Did I bring this about? Am I really unstable? Do I know what I want?" This can go on and on.

We sometimes assume that, if these questions are thought about long and hard enough, and if our feelings are examined in sufficient detail and depth, answers to our problems will emerge. However, Skinner's approach suggests that we are "putting the cart before the horse" when we expect our feelings to explain what's going on in our lives. Instead, if we look closely at existing conditions and at the positive and negative outcomes of our behaviors, we'll find out not only why we are behaving as we are but also why we feel as we do. If there are subtle or hidden meanings to be discovered, these meanings are less likely to be found by intense introspection and tireless self-examination than by careful observation of the environmental circumstances and events affecting us.

Rather than blaming ourselves and engaging in persistent self-analyses when our relationships are in trouble, it is better to focus on questions such as: What specifically is it that each of us does that is aversive to the other (causing him or her to escape or avoid the relationship)? Do we show appreciation (give reinforcement) when one does something that the other likes? Do we ignore (extinguish) each other at times when we should be paying attention (giving reinforcement) to each other? What circumstances serve to strengthen (reinforce) our intimate and loving behaviors? What circumstances serve to suppress (punish) such behaviors? What positive outcomes (reinforcers) are we getting from staying together? What positive outcomes exist outside the relationship?

These types of questions direct attention to the actual sources of many problems. The answers relate to events that are more external and objective than what happens to be going on inside our heads at a particular time (that is, the complex mixture of feelings and thoughts that are resulting from what is happening to us). Therefore the answers provide a more solid basis for evaluating the good and bad points of the relationship and, most importantly, suggest specific ways in which changes for the better might be made. They provide something concrete with which to work. Does this mean that the relationship will be saved? Not necessarily. It depends on the actual positive reinforcers and aversive conditions that exist and on the effects of the behavioral changes that are made. In cases in which more reinforcements occur elsewhere, or in which aversive conditions cannot be changed significantly, the relationship is not likely to survive.

What about the breakup of a relationship and the accompanying feelings of inadequacy, insecurity, anger, and so on? I believe that the same analysis as above applies here. You can dwell on these feelings, or you can focus on the conditions that produce them. If you do the latter, then you are more likely to be able to change conditions so that you experience better feelings. Using a personal example from many years ago, my immediate response to the breakup of my first marriage was one of loss, loneliness, and doubts about the future. Fortunately, events occurred to prevent me from continuing a lot of wasteful and depressing introspection and self-examination (which I had done much of before the separation). After our separation I began a short, but reinforcing, new relationship, intensified some old friendships and started some new ones, and got heavily involved in work and in my university graduate studies. I feel very lucky, in retrospect. This was years before I developed a strong interest in Skinnerian psychology, so I wasn't "planning" my behaviors according to a behavioristic model. It just so happened that I was fortunate. My environment was one that was rich in potential reinforcers, and therefore new behaviors were relatively easily shaped and maintained.

Because of this and many later experiences (not the least of which has been Skinner's influence), I have come to believe that environmental events dominate our feelings. More and more I find myself in agreement with the Skinnerian idea that *feelings are effects, rather than causes,* and therefore it doesn't pay to keep searching within ourselves for answers to our problems. When we are depressed or anxious or have other unpleasant emotions, we should look for the relevant environmental conditions (such as lack of positive reinforcement for our behaviors or the presence of aversive stimuli) that produce these feelings. It is by altering these conditions that we are most likely to get rid of negative feelings and produce positive ones. (Biochemical factors sometimes may need to be considered as well; presently it is unclear to what extent they operate independently from environmental conditions.)

The Immediacy and Importance of Feelings

Technically, feelings can be considered as stimuli that arise within our bodies. They are related to various environmental events, such as reinforcement or punishment for some behavior. We learn from others during the socialization process to label these stimuli as "joy, anxiety," "sadness," and so on, depending on the circumstances under which they occur.

Why do we have strong tendencies to assign major importance to our feelings and to ruminate about them instead of paying more attention to the objective environmental conditions and behaviors of which they are products? A significant reason is because they are so immediate. Feelings are "right here," whereas objective events that are reinforcing or punishing are happening "out there." There are many subtle behaviors, reinforcements, and punishments that are likely to escape our attention as we focus on our feelings. We often get taken up with the feelings themselves, which of course is very nice when they are pleasurable. However, when a feeling is negative, or when we would like to reproduce the conditions that give us positive feelings, it is the environment that needs investigating. It's not unusual to hear someone say something like "I was feeling so great, and then things just seemed to fall apart. I really feel down, and I'm not sure what to do." In such cases a healthy dose of behaviorism can be helpful.

How does someone become a Skinnerian-type behaviorist, focusing on objective behaviors and consequences? In the same way that other behaviors are learned: through experience. As indicated earlier, if reading this book causes you to focus more on your environment, and this way of behaving is then reinforced (perhaps by alleviating some problem), you'll be on the road to becoming more behavioristic. An essential aspect of this approach involves "testing out" behaviors. I've often found it more efficient and effective to get direct feedback from the environment by actually doing something than to continue to ponder what the outcomes of behaviors *might* be. Sometimes, of course, the behavioral consequences are negative, but that isn't necessarily bad. In order to avoid such consequences again, I do something else, which might be reinforced. What I'm suggesting is that more action and less unproductive ruminating (as occurs, for example, when we have had no experiences that allow us to predict consequences) are generally in order. Though I still ruminate too much, I've been weaned away from that approach to a considerable extent by the reinforcements I've gotten for being more behavior oriented.

I want to make it clear that what I've said about feelings is not meant to negate their significance. We live with them, and it's important to most of us that we experience positive ones. A Skinnerian analysis, it seems to me, makes it more likely that we will be able to live fully and enjoyably. By understanding how our behaviors, their consequences, and surrounding conditions (again, contingencies of reinforcement) affect our feelings, we can maximize constructive behaviors and positive emotions.

It's obvious that many persons have a great deal of trouble clearly identifying what they are feeling at various times; they also often seem unsure of what actions to take. These confused feelings and uncertain behaviors can result from inconsistent histories of reinforcement. For example, if in a particular type of situation a behavior results in punishment at one time and reinforcement the next, the individual is bound to experience confused feelings and act in uncertain ways.

A vivid and distressing example of this occurred many years ago when I was sitting in a laundromat waiting for my clothes to finish drying. A woman was there with her son, who looked to be about 5 or 6 years old. The boy would cling to his mother for a time, and she would then begin to tell him to stop acting like a baby and eventually slap him several times, causing him to retreat to a corner of the laundromat. She would then call him back, hug him, and tell him that he was a good boy. After a few minutes of the boy's clinging to her, the cycle would start again: more chastising by the mother, several slaps, the boy retreating, the mother calling him back, and so on. I wondered about this boy's prospects. If this kind of treatment was common in his life, how would he ever develop a set of consistent feelings and behaviors? Mood swings and indecisive actions would seem to be predictable outcomes of his experiences with his erratic mother.

Though this type of dramatically inconsistent experience probably isn't common, more subtle inconsistencies are part of the lives of most of us and cause varying degrees of confused feelings and uncertainties in behavior. We are fortunate when we have enough consistency of positive reinforcement in our everyday lives—in social situations, at home, on the job, and so on—to develop fairly well-defined feelings and confident behaviors. Some persons, however, may have to seek out special situations, such as psychotherapy or behavior therapy, in order to straighten out their feelings and behaviors.

Though the methods used by various therapists differ, a common aspect of many approaches is to provide a consistent, predictable environment within the therapy setting. This type of environment may be precisely what many troubled persons need, since it can serve to steady confused feelings and cause individuals to become increasingly sure of what they are experiencing from within, while also producing more certain behaviors. Both feelings *and* behaviors will be affected if the therapy is successful. (Remember, however, that a behavioristic analysis does not attribute behavioral changes to changed feelings. Contrary to what many therapists believe, radical behaviorists maintain that the environment ultimately exerts control. The "environment" in this case includes the therapeutic setting, the therapist's behaviors, the consequences of the client's behaviors, and so on—these environmental conditions are related to whatever improvements occur in the client's emotional states and overt behavioral responses.)

What I am suggesting here is consistent with Skinner's assertion that feelings are effects, not causes. I believe that we need to experience fairly consistent feelings (effects) for similar behaviors in similar circumstances in order to be "well adjusted." Some degree of emotional stability is essential to our well-being, and this stability results from reasonably consistent histories of reinforcement. Putting this in simple terms, we need reliable love and affection from those with whom we are intimately involved, reliable positive outcomes for good work performance, and so on. There is nothing new in these recommendations. However, from a Skinnerian perspective, we can see even more clearly that consistent behaviors and emotional states are related to consistent consequences and conditions provided by our environments. Erratic environments tend to produce erratic behaviors and feelings.

Skinner's radical behaviorism casts a clear, and often unique, light on many aspects of everyday situations and behaviors. Also, it points out factors that should be obvious to us but that we often ignore. As detailed in the previous pages, it can help us to focus on (1) self-help strategies that involve changing overt behaviors and environmental conditions; (2) the importance of positive reinforcement in interpersonal relations; (3) the long-range futility of blaming others for their annoying, disruptive, or harmful behaviors; (4) the inefficiency of self-blame and intensive self-analysis; and (5) the role that feelings play in our lives. Much of this discussion consists of my own elaborations on Skinner's ideas, but I believe I've remained within his behavioristic framework.

Concluding Comments

Perhaps the aspects of Skinner's psychology that most often are found disturbing are its radical determinism and its emphasis on control. Many persons seem unable to get past these issues to look objectively at other features of Skinner's approach. They simply can't accept that our behaviors are determined and continually controlled by genetic and environmental influences. Admittedly, these are hard pills to swallow. We feel free and able to make choices and decisions about our lives (at least sometimes), and therefore it just doesn't seem to make sense to say that we have no real freedom and are controlled all the time.

I've often thought about the implications of radical determinism, and they are mind-boggling. Although it may represent the way things really are (and essentially I believe that it's true), most of us can't live on a day-to-day basis with this philosophy constantly in mind. To some extent I sympathize with Skinner's critics who suggest that a radically deterministic view makes nonsense of our lives. If ultimate control rests in genetic and environmental influences and we are only "loci" for these influences, what's the use of trying to improve ourselves or the world? Our fates, as well as the fate of society, are sealed by fortunate or unfortunate genetic structures and personal environmental circumstances.

If Skinner's research and writings, as well as the activities of all of us, are determined by conditions that have nothing to do with personal choices and decisions, what meaning can anything have? Because of his genetic endowment and the consequences of various behaviors during his lifetime, Skinner proposed certain ideas, and whether or not we accept his proposals is in turn determined by the genetic endowment and environmental circumstances of each of us. In other words, according to radical determinism, there is no point at which individual free choice enters into the process. To make a long story short, these considerations are nerve-wracking. Complete and constant agreement with radical determinism is impossible for most of us; it's simply too inconsistent with all we have learned as members of this society. (From a deterministic viewpoint, our genes and experiences have determined that we cannot "accept" a completely deterministic philosophy. As you can see, this is a very complicated business.)

Of course, if Skinner's type of determinism is rejected, then the rejector can be asked: "What else, other than genetic and environmental conditions, can determine behavior? If there is something beyond our bodies, with all their component parts, and the physical and social environments within which we function, what is it?" The answer could be "the human spirit," "the will of God," or some other such quality. However, these answers take us out of the naturalistic world of a science of human behavior. (Such qualities may or may not exist; in any case, naturalistic approaches to the study of human behavior cannot systematically take them into account.)

With regard to Skinner's deterministic position, a very important point must be made. It's one that is obvious but sometimes forgotten: his assumptions, as he himself suggested, do not change what actually exists. Whether or not our lives are completely determined is not decided by what Skinner said. Either we live in a wholly determined system or we do not. If we do, it doesn't seem to affect the fact that we are capable of feeling as if were free; nor does it change the feeling that our behaviors are meaningful. Therefore, do we have to be weighed down by heavy philosophical questions about "ultimate reality"? It seems to me that we can simply use Skinner's concepts and strive to change our environments so that productive and beneficial behaviors will increase and feelings of freedom will be enhanced.

When behavioristic procedures such as positive reinforcement are used and are effective, they continue to be used. The important step is getting beyond whatever aversive elements one finds in Skinnerian psychology, and I hope this book has the effect of making that happen. Even those who don't share Skinner's belief that behavior is completely determined by genetic and environmental conditions can find beneficial applications of concepts such as positive reinforcement.

Although nowadays I spend little time concerning myself with whether or not we live in a completely determined world (a question that can't really be answered anyway), I do believe that the most effective way of understanding and changing behavior (my own and others') is to focus on environmental conditions. From this perspective, which is supported by a considerable amount of behavioral-science research, much of what I hear and read about human behavior seems remarkably antiquated. Behaviorists have made substantial advances in recent years, and studies have shown that environmental changes in institutions, schools, businesses, family settings, and so on can bring about beneficial behavioral changes. This often has been accomplished by planning situations in which appropriate positive reinforcement plays a greater role while the use of punishment or aversive control is minimized. At the individual level, also, persons have improved their own lives by applying behavioral procedures.

Despite these advances in knowledge about how environmental circumstances affect behavior, and despite the vast amount of behavioristic literature by Skinner and others, there still remain many persons who talk and write about human behavior as though the evidence and ideas of the behaviorists do not exist. For example, it's doubtful that Freud himself, if he were still alive, would believe what he wrote in the 1920s and 1930s. Yet there are those today who hold orthodox Freudian ideas, or very similar ones, as the last words on human nature and behavior.

Though Skinner's certainly is not the one and only possible interpretation of behavior, it's surprising that his concepts have not been more widely applied. For example, as indicated earlier, just by glancing at recent newspaper and magazine editorials and articles, it's easy to find comments like "the darkness in man's soul that corrupts his best intentions," "the destructive tendencies hidden deep within the human psyche, ready to burst forth at any moment," "the failing American character that is bringing us to the edge of national disaster," "the lack of morality and willpower among our citizens," and so on.

The tone of certainty in many such statements makes it clear that the writers have been untouched by the possibility that environmental influences (rather than dark souls, hidden destructive tendencies, failing characters, or moral and willpower deficiencies) are primarily responsible for our problems. This focus on inner causes detracts from analyses of the effects of our political, economic, educational, legal, and other social institutions on our behaviors. Also, it directs our attention away from the multitude of environmental conditions that affect our day-to-day lives on the job, at home, with our friends, and elsewhere.

Analyzing our environments and changing them so that positive reinforcement becomes the rule rather than the exception, and so that punitive and aversive controls are minimized, would constitute a tough, time-consuming job. Perhaps that is a major reason why many people continue to explain human behavior in antiquated ways. It's quick and easy to blame our behavioral problems on something that is out of sight, such as a "dark soul" or a "moral deficiency." Also, we provide reinforcement for these types of explanations by agreeing with them: Person number one says "The country is going to the dogs because no one has any moral fiber." And person number two replies "Yes, you're right. No one seems to care anymore." This is an easy interaction, and no long, drawn-out explanations of environmental influences are required. Of course, those influences also go unexamined and unchanged.

Reading and rereading Skinner's writings remains of interest to me, despite the fact that I've been doing so on and off for many years. One of the main reasons is that his ideas, though sometimes extended considerably beyond his research findings, are nevertheless grounded in that research. He had, at some level, a sound basis for his suggestions. He spent many years in the experimental laboratory, and important findings have been applied in the world outside the laboratory. He was no "armchair philosopher."

Also, I continue to find nuggets of practical wisdom in Skinner's writings (which are among the reinforcers that keep me reading his books and articles). For example, in an article in the magazine *Human Nature* (Skinner, 1978b, p. 91), he explained that it isn't the possession of goods, but rather the effective action that produces the goods, that makes us happy. He also suggested that we are mistaken when we believe that others will be happy if we simply give them good things. Their happiness is probable only if the things we give them enable them to take further action. The implication is that, although acquiring things may make people happy, simply possessing them does not. This idea certainly is not brand new or unique, but it is one that is worth being reminded of. It is easy to slip into believing that "Once I get what I want (money, a good job, an expensive house, or whatever), I will be happy." As many persons have found out, getting these things may be much more fun than having them, especially when the possessions fail to lead to other effective and fulfilling behaviors.

Finally, Skinner's radical behaviorism makes me a bit more optimistic about our future possibilities. It's an approach that allows us to escape some of the weight of the often gloomy history of humankind. Each new generation (and, for that matter, each individual) offers renewed possibilities for the improvement of civilization. We aren't necessarily stuck with our current problems; we can improve if the contingencies of reinforcement can be changed. All in all, I believe that Skinner made a major contribution to the possible betterment of an ailing world. Best of all, his procedures and ideas can be used even by those who have doubts about some of his underlying assumptions. We don't have to become "disciples" in order to apply his suggestions and observe the effects.

ANNOTATED
REFERENCES

BROWN, P. L. (1982). *Managing behavior on the job.* New York: Wiley. A practical behavioral
approach to management is described, with many good examples. The basic focus
is on antecedents, behavior, and consequences and is closely related to Skinner's
concept of "contingencies of reinforcement."

CHOMSKY, N. (1959). Review of Skinner's *Verbal Behavior. Language,* Vol. 35, No. 1, pp.
26–58. A critical review of Skinner's 1957 book. Chomsky wrote that Skinner's
"astonishing claims are far from justified" (p. 28). Skinner suggested that Chomsky
misunderstood the behavioral approach, and the controversy continued.

CORDES, C. (1984, November). Easing toward perfection at Twin Oaks: *Walden Two* model
now 17. *APA Monitor,* pp. 1, 30–31. An update on a small community started in
1967 and inspired by Skinner's novel, *Walden Two.*

EPSTEIN, R. (1977). A listing of the published works of B. F. Skinner, with notes and comments.
Behaviorism, Vol. 5, No. 1, pp. 99–110.

EPSTEIN, R. (1987). In the yellow wood. In S. Modgil & C. Modgil (Eds.), *B. F. Skinner:
Consensus and controversy* (pp. 333–335). New York: Falmer. The case for a
science of behavior separate from the traditional field of psychology is stated
briefly. Epstein indicates Skinner's "significant contributions to the scientific
understanding of behavior" (p. 333).

EPSTEIN, R., & SKINNER, B. F. (1982). *Skinner for the classroom: Selected papers.* Champaign,
IL: Research Press. Epstein discusses eight common misunderstandings regarding
Skinner; then 15 of Skinner's most widely cited papers are presented, each with
an introduction and a postscript. Also, there is a list of Skinner's publications as
of December 1981.

EVANS, R. I. (1968). *B. F. Skinner: The man and his ideas.* New York: Dutton. A book-length
interview in which Skinner informally answers questions about Freud, aversive
versus positive methods of control, education, the role of theories, misunderstandings and misinterpretations of his approach, and other topics.

FERSTER, C. B., & Skinner, B. F. (1957). *Schedules of reinforcement.* New York: Appleton-Century-Crofts. A detailed empirical examination of the effects of many different reinforcement patterns.

FREUD, S. (1965). *New introductory lectures on psychoanalysis.* New York: Norton. First published in 1933, this book contains seven lectures covering a variety of psychoanalytic issues.

FREUD, S. (1969). *An outline of psycho-analysis.* New York: Norton. Originally published in 1940, this is Freud's last book. It is a concise overview of psychoanalytic theory.

GOODELL, R. (1975, August). The visible scientist. *APA Monitor,* pp. 1, 8. A study in which 82% of college students could identify Skinner.

HALL, C. S. (1954). *A primer of Freudian psychology.* New York: New American Library. A brief, widely known summary of Freudian theory.

HALL, E. (1972, November). Will success spoil B. F. Skinner? *Psychology Today,* pp. 65–72, 130. A wide-ranging interview in which Skinner talks about his work and its applications, the concepts of freedom and dignity, *Walden Two,* artistic behaviors, and more.

HALL, M. H. (1967, September). An interview with "Mr. Behaviorist"—B. F. Skinner. *Psychology Today,* pp. 21–23, 68–71. A lively interview in which he comments on religion, childrearing, his critics, and other subjects.

HOLLAND, J. G., & Skinner, B. F. (1961). *The analysis of behavior: A program for self-instruction.* New York: McGraw-Hill. A programmed textbook that presents the basic terms and principles of the scientific analysis of behavior. "This book is itself one application of the science" (p. vii).

HOMANS, G. C. (1977, July–August). A conversation with B. F. Skinner, psychologist. *Harvard Magazine,* pp. 53–58. Homans, a distinguished Harvard sociologist, informally questions Skinner about his background, his scientific assumptions, teaching machines, *Walden Two,* the Aircrib that he used with his second daughter, and other interesting matters.

KAZDIN, A. E. (1989). *Behavior modification in applied settings* (4th ed.). Pacific Grove, CA: Brooks/Cole. An introduction to behavior-modification techniques in various settings, with a major (though not exclusive) focus on operant-conditioning approaches.

KELLER, F. S. (1990, Winter) Burrhus Frederick Skinner (1904–1990) (A thank-you). *Journal of Applied Behavior Analysis,* Vol. 23, No. 4, pp. 404–408. A brief remembrance by Skinner's long-term friend and associate. Skinner and Keller met in graduate school at Harvard.

KLEIN, S. B. (1987). *Learning: Principles and applications.* New York: McGraw-Hill. Contains a brief comparison of Skinner's view of language acquisition with that of Noam Chomsky, the famous linguist and noted critic of Skinner (pp. 345–348 and 353).

LIPSITT, L. (1990, December). Science directions: Nurture is what affects whether or not the genes get to "play out." *APA Monitor,* p. 13. A brief, clearly stated perspective on the nature-nurture issue.

MARTIN, G., & PEAR, J. (1988). *Behavior modification: What it is and how to do it* (3rd ed.). Englewood Cliffs, NJ: Prentice-Hall. An introduction to behavior modification principles and tactics, designed primarily for students and practitioners.

MODGIL, S., & MODGIL, C. (Eds.). (1987) *B. F. Skinner: Consensus and controversy.* New York: Falmer. A number of complex and detailed issues related to Skinner's approach are debated by distinguished academics. Considerable background information is required to comprehend fully the arguments made.

NYE, R. D. (1992). *Three psychologies: Perspectives from Freud, Skinner, and Rogers* (4th ed.). Pacific Grove, CA: Brooks/Cole. The essential ideas of Freud, Skinner, and Rogers are presented and then compared, contrasted, and criticized.

PERLMAN, D. (1980, January). Who's who in psychology. *American Psychologist.* Vol. 35, No. 1, pp. 104–106. Includes a study in which Skinner ranked second (Freud was first) in number of citations in a sample of introductory psychology textbooks.

POWELL, D. A. (1987, April). Cognitive and affective components of reinforcement. *American Psychologist,* Vol. 42, No. 4, pp. 409–410. A commentary on "What Is Wrong with Daily Life in the Western World?" (Skinner, 1986).

PROCTOR, R. W., & Weeks, D. J. (1990). *The goal of B. F. Skinner and behavior analysis.* (New York: Springer-Verlag. A very critical review of Skinner and his approach. Questions are raised about the scientific support for Skinner's proposals, and he and his colleagues are accused of dogmatism. Many of the points in the book are controversial.

ROGERS, C. R. (1959) A theory of therapy, personality, and interpersonal relationships, as developed in the client-centered framework. In S. Koch (Ed.), *Psychology: A study of a science* (Vol. 3), pp. 184–256. New York: McGraw-Hill. The most complete and detailed presentation available of Rogers's theoretical assumptions.

ROGERS, C. R. (1961). *On becoming a person.* Boston: Houghton Mifflin. A wide-ranging collection of Rogers's papers, expressing his views on psychotherapy, research, and everyday-life situations.

ROGERS, C. R. (1964). Toward a science of the person. In T. W. Wann (Ed.), *Behaviorism and phenomenology,* pp. 109–140. Chicago: University of Chicago Press. Rogers presents his approach to the study of human behavior, which incorporates subjective, objective, and interpersonal knowledge.

ROGERS, C. R. (1969). Freedom to learn. Columbus, OH: Merrill. Rogers's views on teaching, learning, and the educational system are presented. An updated version is *Freedom to Learn for the 80's,* published in 1983.

ROGERS, C. R. (1980) *A way of being.* Boston: Houghton Mifflin. Fifteen chapters cover Rogers's personal experiences and perspectives, the person-centered approach, education, and the future.

ROGERS, C. R., & Skinner, B. F. (1956, November 30). Some issues concerning the control of human behavior. *Science,* Vol. 124, No. 3231, pp. 1057–1066. The well-known confrontation between Rogers and Skinner at a symposium held by the American Psychological Association. Each expressed his views, with the topic of how values emerge being a primary issue.

ROHTER, L. (1989, November 7). Isolated desert community lives by Skinner's precepts. *New York Times,* pp. C1, C8. Los Horcones, Mexico, a community influenced by Skinner's concepts, is the subject.

SKINNER, B. F. (1938). *The behavior of organisms: An experimental analysis.* New York: Appleton-Century-Crofts. His early experimental studies of behavior, using rats as subjects, are presented.

SKINNER, B. F. (1948). *Walden two.* New York: Macmillan. A novel about a utopian community based on the application of behavioral-science concepts. Widely read and much discussed, this work of fiction continues to stimulate, and sometimes irritate, its readers.

SKINNER, B. F. (1953). *Science and human behavior.* New York: Macmillan. Perhaps the best and most complete general introduction to his position. Covers a wide range of topics: the role of a science of human behavior, the analysis of behavior, self-control, thinking, social behavior, government and law, religion, psychotherapy, education, cultural design, and more.

SKINNER, B. F. (1957). *Verbal behavior.* New York: Appleton-Century-Crofts. Skinner's attempt to analyze language using his operant approach.

SKINNER, B. F. (1961, November). Teaching machines. *Scientific American,* pp. 90–102. A brief description of teaching machines and their advantages.

SKINNER, B. F. (1963, May 31). Behaviorism at fifty. *Science,* Vol. 140, No. 3570, pp. 951–958. A difficult article but one worth studying. It states the case for a behavioristic philosophy of science and deals in some detail with the topic of conscious experiencing. Reprinted in *Contingencies of Reinforcement* (Skinner, 1969a).

SKINNER, B. F. (1967). Autobiography. In E. G. Boring & G. Lindzey (Eds.), *A history of psychology in autobiography* (Vol. 5), pp. 385–413. New York: Irvington. A brief, interesting overview of his life, beginning with his childhood in Susquehanna, Pennsylvania. Reveals major influences on his behavior.

SKINNER, B. F. (1968) *The technology of teaching.* New York: Appleton-Century-Crofts. Describes the applications of his approach to problems of teaching and learning.

SKINNER, B. F. (1969a). *Contingencies of reinforcement: A theoretical analysis.* Englewood Cliffs, NJ: Prentice-Hall. Nine chapters cover weighty theoretical issues related to contingencies of reinforcement and cultural design, the analysis of ontogenic and phylogenic contingencies, and a critique of alternative theories.

SKINNER, B. F. (1969b, April). The machine that is man. *Psychology Today,* pp. 20–25, 60–63. An intriguing discussion of various views of the causes of human behavior and the complexities of comparing humans and machines.

SKINNER, B. F. (1971). *Beyond freedom and dignity.* New York: Knopf. A direct challenge to traditional concepts of freedom and dignity. Calls for a technological approach to solving social problems, discusses alternatives to the widespread use of punishment, investigates values, suggests that cultural design be employed, asks "What is man?" and raises other important issues. This book has received a great deal of publicity and is very controversial.

SKINNER, B. F. (1972). *Cumulative record: A selection of papers* (3rd ed.). New York: Appleton-Century-Crofts. A collection of 48 articles covering various topics, including the concept of freedom, experimental methodology, education, psychoanalysis, psychoses, creativity, literary and verbal behavior, superstitious behavior, and theoretical matters.

SKINNER, B. F. (1973a). Answers for my critics. In H. Wheeler (Ed.), *Beyond the punitive society,* pp. 256–266. San Francisco: W. H. Freeman. An excellent short article that addresses major misunderstandings of Skinner's science of behavior and its uses.

SKINNER, B. F. (1973b). Humanism and behaviorism. In F. W. Matson (Ed.), *Without/within: Behaviorism and humanism,* pp. 47–53. Pacific Grove, CA: Brooks/Cole. A brief, clear statement of Skinner's position versus humanistic psychology's emphasis on the inner person. Reprinted in *Reflections on Behaviorism and Society* (Skinner, 1978a). This article first appeared in *The Humanist,* July/August 1972.

SKINNER, B. F. (1974). *About behaviorism.* New York: Knopf. A wide-ranging work in which he attempts to correct 20 common misconceptions of his approach and covers topics such as the "world within the skin," innate behavior, verbal behavior, thinking, motivation and emotion, the self, and the question of control.

SKINNER, B. F. (1975, January). The steep and thorny way to a science of behavior. *American Psychologist,* Vol. 30, No. 1, pp. 42–49. He briefly explains again his views on behavioral science, the role of feelings and "inner determinants," the importance of focusing on environmental conditions, and other issues. The central theme is that we are being diverted from a scientific approach to human behavior. Reprinted in *Reflections on Behaviorism and Society* (Skinner, 1978a).

SKINNER, B. F. (1976). *Particulars of my life.* New York: Knopf. An interesting autobiographical account, it is the first in a three-volume series. Traces his development from childhood to his entrance into the graduate psychology program at Harvard University. Includes fascinating details about growing up in a small northeastern town shortly after the turn of the century. He continued the story of his life in *The Shaping of a Behaviorist* (1979b) and *A Matter of Consequences* (1983b).

SKINNER, B. F. (1977, September). Between freedom and despotism. *Psychology Today,* pp. 80–91. A discussion of the importance of person-to-person positive reinforcement as a means of governing social problems.

SKINNER, B. F. (1978a). *Reflections on behaviorism and society.* Englewood Cliffs, NJ: Prentice-Hall. An excellent collection of 18 papers on a variety of topics, including "Human Behavior and Democracy," "The Ethics of Helping People," "Humanism and Behaviorism," "Walden Two Revisited," "Why I Am Not a Cognitive Psychologist," and "The Free and Happy Student."

SKINNER, B. F. (1978b, March). Why don't we use the behavioral sciences? *Human Nature,* pp. 86–92. An exceptionally clear and concise treatment of his views on the need for a behavioral-science approach to social problems and the uselessness of looking within the person for explanations of behavior.

SKINNER, B. F. (1979a, March). My experience with the baby-tender. *Psychology Today,* pp. 28–31, 34, 37–38, 40. Relates the story of the development and use of the baby-tender, or Aircrib, about which there are so many rumors. Skinner's younger daughter, Deborah, spent time in the Aircrib during her infancy; she seems to have had a normal childhood and to have become a normal adult. For more information, see "Baby in a Box," pp. 269–276 in *Skinner for the Classroom* (Epstein & Skinner, 1982) or pp. 567–573 in *Cumulative Record,* 3rd ed. (Skinner, 1972).

SKINNER, B. F. (1979b). *The shaping of a behaviorist: Part two of an autobiography.* New York: Knopf. The second volume of a three-volume autobiography, it begins with his graduate-student days at Harvard and ends with his return there, 20 years later, as a professor.

SKINNER, B. F. (1983a, March). Intellectual self-management in old age. *American Psychologist,* Vol. 38, No. 3, pp. 239–244. Skinner applies his behavioral approach to problems of aging and offers his own personal techniques for coping with these problems. Reprinted in *Upon Further Reflection* (Skinner, 1987a).

SKINNER, B. F. (1983b). *A matter of consequences: Part three of an autobiography.* New York: Knopf. The third volume of a three-volume autobiography, it begins with his return to Harvard in 1948 as Professor of Psychology and presents details of his life and work up to the early 1980s.

SKINNER, B. F. (1983c, September). Origins of a behaviorist. *Psychology Today,* pp. 22–33. Skinner reflects on his life, his work, and the writing of his autobiography. Sections on education and creativity, and a "Skinner sampler," also are included.

SKINNER, B. F. (1984, September). The shame of American education. *American Psychologist,* Vol. 39, No. 9, pp. 947–954. Specific recommendations are made for changing our educational system, including greater use of programmed instruction and training of teachers to be more effective. Reprinted in *Upon Further Reflection* (Skinner, 1987a).

SKINNER, B. F. (1986, May). What is wrong with daily life in the Western World? *American Psychologist,* Vol. 41, No. 5, pp. 568–574. "Human behavior in the West has grown weak, but it can be strengthened through the use of principles derived from an experimental analysis of behavior" (p. 568). Reprinted in *Upon Further Reflection* (Skinner, 1987a).

SKINNER, B. F. (1987a). *Upon further reflection.* Englewood Cliffs, NJ: Prentice-Hall. Fourteen articles are presented; the major topics cover global issues, the origins of behavior, current issues in psychology and education, behavioral self-management, and issues of concern to behavior analysts. The central theme is "the commitment to an experimental analysis of behavior and its use in the interpretation of human affairs" (p. vii).

SKINNER, B. F. (1987b, August). Whatever happened to psychology as the science of behavior? *American Psychologist,* Vol. 42, No. 8, pp. 780–786. A criticism of psychology—especially humanistic psychology, psychotherapy, and cognitive psychology— for remaining concerned primarily with internal determinants of behavior. The experimental analysis of behavior is suggested as the remedy. Reprinted in *Recent Issues in the Analysis of Behavior* (Skinner, 1989).

SKINNER, B. F. (1988, June). A statement on punishment. *APA Monitor,* p. 22. Skinner suggests that limited, specific uses of punishment sometimes may be justified, but nonpunitive alternatives should always be sought.

SKINNER, B. F. (1989). *Recent issues in the analysis of behavior.* Columbus, OH: Merrill. Twelve articles are included, addressed primarily to psychologists and behavior analysts. Most of the volume concerns theoretical and professional issues.

SKINNER, B. F. (1990a, November). Can psychology be a science of the mind? *American Psychologist,* Vol. 45, No. 11, pp. 1206–1210. This article, on which Skinner worked until the evening before his death, continues his criticisms of cognitive psychology and supports the experimental analysis of behavior.

SKINNER, B. F. (1990b, Fall). To know the future. *The Behavior Analyst,* Vol. 13, No. 2, pp. 103–106. "Knowledge by description" and "knowledge by acquaintance" are discussed, as they relate to future changes in our culture. Skinner again expresses his concerns about current world problems.

SKINNER, B. F., & VAUGHAN, M. E. (1983). *Enjoy old age: Living fully in your later years.* New York: Warner. A short book with large print, it presents perspectives on aging and recommends practical solutions to the problems of growing old (based largely on Skinner's own approaches to these problems).

STAATS, A. W. (1988, September). Skinner's theory and the emotion-behavior relationship: Incipient change with major implications. *American Psychologist,* Vol. 43, No. 9, pp. 747–748. Another commentary on "What Is Wrong with Daily Life in the Western World?" (Skinner, 1986).

TIME STAFF. (1971, September 20). Skinner's utopia: Panacea, or path to Hell. *Time,* pp. 47–53. An interesting popular article on his life and work and on the controversies that he generated.

VARGAS, J. S. (1990, Winter). B. F. Skinner—The last few days. *Journal of Applied Behavior Analysis,* Vol. 23, No. 4, pp. 409–410. A touching account of Skinner's final days, written by his older daughter.

VAUGHAN, M. E. (1990, Fall). Reflections on B. F. Skinner. *The Behavior Analyst,* Vol. 13, No. 2, pp. 101–102. A brief remembrance by a close friend and associate. Some small, interesting details are revealed, including Skinner's annoying "compulsion to give directions" (p. 102) when someone else was driving.

WATSON, D. L., & THARP, R. G. (1989). *Self-directed behavior: Self-modification for personal adjustment* (5th ed.). Pacific Grove, CA: Brooks/Cole. Presents a general theory of behavior, exercises for self-analysis, and "concrete information on how to achieve the goals you hold for yourself" (p. vii). The focus is not specifically Skinnerian; a variety of self-change strategies are presented.

WATSON, J. B., & RAYNER, R. (1920, February). Conditioned emotional reactions. *Journal of Experimental Psychology,* Vol. 3, pp. 1–14. The well-known study in which 11-month-old "little Albert" was conditioned to fear a white rat. It is a controversial study with regard to procedures, ethics, and interpretations.

WRIGHT, G. D. (1970, July). A further note on ranking the important psychologists. *American Psychologist,* Vol. 25, No. 7, pp. 650–651. Briefly explains a survey in which Skinner was ranked first among contemporary contributors to psychology.

INDEX

Index

Index